Coping with College

Coping with College

A Guide for Academic Success

Alice L. Hamachek
Central Michigan University

Allyn and Bacon
Boston • London • Toronto • Sydney • Tokyo • Singapore

Copyright © 1995 by Allyn & Bacon
A Simon & Schuster Company
Needham Heights, Massachusetts 02194

Library of Congress Cataloging-in-Publication Data

Hamachek, Alice L.
    Coping with college : a guide for academic success / Alice L. Hamachek.
        p.   cm.
    Includes bibliographical references and index.
    ISBN 0–205–16579–6
    1.   College student orientation--Handbooks, manuals, etc.   2.   Study
skills--Handbooks, manuals, etc.   3.   Motivation in education—
—Handbooks, manuals, etc.   I. Title.
    LB2343.3.H36 1995
    378.1'98--dc20   94–19866
                                                                            CIP

Printed in the United States of America
10 9 8 7 6 5 4 3 2 1   98 97 96 95 94

Dedication

With love and appreciation, I dedicate this book to. . .

*My wonderful family and friends, who encouraged me
to climb the rainbows of my dreams!*

*My faithful companions, Molly and Mutzi,
who quietly took catnaps while I wrote this book!*

*My fantastic students, who are discovering the joy
of striving for excellence!*

Contents

Preface

Coping with College: A Guide for Academic Success is a handy book for the person who is interested in achieving academic excellence in educational endeavors. The book is filled with practical suggestions for the action-oriented student who functions in a fast-paced world that values excellence. The book contains key elements that form the foundational framework for outstanding achievement in higher level academic settings.

The style of this book is informal and the tone is friendly. The language is interactive and conversational. The information in this book can be easily applied to a variety of learning situations. The approach to learning is positive and suggests that studying can be an enjoyable experience when success is a probability.

Clinical and classroom settings provided the background experiences for this book. Research for the content was conducted over a period of years and included interviews with a multitude of students from throughout the United States. Therefore, suggestions in this book represent the knowledge of years of study, the wisdom of years of teaching, and the advice of students who were actually encountering the daily challenges of college life.

Each section is written so it can be used independently or blended with the other sections to form an integrated whole. The independent nature of each section allows the student to target particular areas and get needed information without reading the entire text. The text is organized to make specific information readily accessible so it can be instantaneously applied.

Coping with College encourages the student to become actively involved in the content and application of skills and strategies for academic success. The student is given direct instruction related to the topics presented. In addition, guidelines for enhancing one's depth of knowledge and understanding are included. Therefore, one can do as little or as much as necessary to accomplish the desired outcome.

It has been said that *success is a journey*. Thus, if academic triumph and good fortune occur frequently, the journey, though it may be long and difficult, will be much more enjoyable. Believe in yourself! Magnificent possibilities are abundant and you have great potential! Accept the challenge and claim the victory!

Matriculation!

CONGRATULATIONS! You have met all the requirements to become matriculated at the University!

1. Start packing!
2. Tell your friends!
3. Leave the dog at home!
4. Bring your checkbook!
5. Buy an organizer!
6. Get a physical!
7. Sell your high school jersey!
8. Pay your tuition!
9. Clean your room!
10. Get ready! Get set! Go for it!

Coping with College

1

College

The Demands of College

The demands of college are significantly different from those of
high school. The academic curriculum, the rigors of academic expectations and evaluations, the resources available, your particular course of study, and your performance in high school are all fac-
tors that will play a part in determining the challenge of your
transition from high school to college.

Also, this transition may be more difficult if you are going from
a small high school to a large university. The larger the university,
the more complex the organizational and physical structure and
this alone will put additional strains on your organizational, spatial, and social skills.

Although the specific differences between high school and college will vary depending on your particular situation, the following
list will alert you to some major considerations that will likely impact your transition and adjustment. This list is an effort to help
you cope with some of the problems and pitfalls before they conquer you.

1. Size of the College Campus

The size of the college campus can be intimidating. The confines of
the single building of the traditional high school become vastly different on a university campus that may span hundreds of acres.

One familiar building must be exchanged for many buildings that may be far apart, look quite similar, and have a number of levels and intricate architectural floor plans.

For example, if you have spatial, directional, or orientation difficulties, you may experience some problems. It may be difficult for you to organize your schedule to be able to get from one class to another in the time allotted for class transition. If you have a bad sense of direction, you may find yourself late for classes because you end up in the wrong building or room. You may get to your classroom and find that the location has been changed and you don't know where the new location is.

2. Size of Some Classes

In college, some classes may have more than 100 students enrolled. Often these classes are held in large lecture halls or auditoriums. Students may not have seat assignments, thus, you may never be seated next to the same person throughout the term. It may be difficult to meet other students who you know well enough to feel comfortable studying with or consulting if you have questions or concerns.

Some large classes may be taught by a person or the instruction may be via television, video, or other forms of educational technology. If a large class is taught by a person, it may be one professor, several professors, or a team of professor and graduate assistants. Consequently, you may find it more difficult to establish a relationship with your instructor or to have that instructor know you by name and face.

Large class formats may present problems with seeing the visual aids and hearing the audio portion of the lecture. You may not have a choice of seating location and may find yourself at the back of the room with no other option for relocating.

Also, it may be much harder for you to concentrate since there likely will be many more distractions. With large groups there likely will be more moving about, more coughing, more talking, and even more goofing off ! Since college professors don't expect to have to enforce discipline, some students may take this opportunity to socialize and consequently cause you to be distracted from the task at hand.

3. Schedule of Daily Classes

In college, the daily schedule of classes is more diverse than it was in high school. In high school, the daily schedule was probably the same every day or close to it. In college, classes are structured differently. You may have some classes that meet for one hour on Monday, Wednesday, and Friday, others that meet for ninety minutes on Tuesday and Thursday, or a night class that meets for three hours in a single block. Interspersed may be a lab session that meets periodically. These are some traditional ways in which classes are organized. Thus, your daily schedule may be very different than the one you probably experienced in high school.

Your concentration and ability to stay on task may be taxed to the limit in the longer class sessions and on days when you have more hours of classes. In addition, the class schedule will be completely different as semesters or terms change and you will have to readjust to a new time frame and different classes.

This less structured hourly schedule may create problems for the student who is not aware of the pitfalls. Since you will not have classes scheduled every hour on the hour, you will have to use some of that time to study. Consequently, it will be important that you program your day with classes and study periods so you don't trick your brain into believing that since you have attended your class sessions, you don't have anything else to do.

4. Independence

Independence is wonderful, however, don't forget it requires a great deal of responsibility! If you get behind, it is HARD TO GET CAUGHT UP! Balance independence and responsibility wisely. You won't be sorry.

Why Am I Going to/in College?

There are many reasons why a person chooses to go to college. Some of them might be considered "good" reasons while others might be considered "bad" reasons. Regardless, the commitment you make to being a successful college student will likely reflect the reasons behind your decision to attend college.

© 1989, 1991, 1992 Joel Pett, Lexington Herald-Leader. Reprinted by Permission.

Use the following list to stimulate your thinking and to focus on your feelings and purpose for being in college. If your thought or feeling is not included, use the space provided to list your own.

College Is:

1. A place to party!
2. A place to train myself so I can get a good job.
3. A way to get away from home.
4. An opportunity to develop more of my potential.
5. A better alternative to getting a job or going into the military service.
6. The best chance of obtaining the kind of life I desire in the future.
7. A chance to participate in athletics.
8. What my parents want.
9. What I want.
10. The fulfillment of a dream.

11. A chance to begin again.
12. A place to find a mate.
13. _____

Once you have specified your main reason for attending college, think about its compatibility with intensive academic study. If it is not compatible, you may need to prepare yourself for difficulties when it comes report card time! Or, you could change your perspective.

Getting a good college education requires a commitment to academic excellence. Remember, it's tougher to catch up than it is to keep up.

Becoming an Independent Learner

The life style and academic rigors of college life require a great sense of discipline as an independent learner. In college, there is no one to get you to your classes, to see that you are not late, to be sure that you have done your homework, or to help you with personal chores such as doing your laundry, cleaning your room, and paying your bills.

Becoming an independent learner takes some time, and it also requires some skills. The following are some suggestions to help you focus your energy on becoming an independent learner and experiencing academic success.

1. Know your goals
2. Keep organized
3. Learn what motivates you
4. Establish an effective study area
5. Use all your senses for learning
6. Recognize the importance of rehearsal and review
7. Believe that you can be successful
8. Enhance your level of aspiration
9. Demonstrate responsibility for your learning
10. Develop higher level thinking skills
11. Seek opportunities to learn
12. Cultivate an open mind
13. Read widely
14. Take studying seriously

Becoming a More Effective Student

Your job in college is to be a student. Most likely you will want to be a good one!

The goal of all educational instruction is learning. Learning is commonly defined as a change of behavior. You likely have learned how to tie you shoes, write your name, and drive a car. These were things that at one time you did not know how to do. However, your behavior changed and, thus, you learned! You now know how to do those things.

For the most part, the problem isn't learning. You have great ability to learn or you wouldn't have made it to college! It is more probable that academic problems occur when learning isn't effective or efficient.

How do you become a more efficient and effective student? Here are some general principles. Mastering these principles

will be among the most important accomplishments that you ever experience.

1. Spend Time Studying

Many students think that they are spending lots of time studying. However, study time includes only the time spent on the task. It does not include the time you spend getting organized, daydreaming, or tuning into distractions.

Time is one of your most important learning resources because it is directly under your control. There are twenty-four hours in each day and that is fixed. You can not add hours to your day. You can only make effective use of the time you have.

Research makes it quite clear that there is no substitute for the amount of time spent studying. An increase in study time is strongly related to an increase in learning. This principle is one of the most important principles you will ever learn. If effectively applied to your studies, it will be invaluable in your quest to be a successful student.

2. Acquire a Wide Range of Learning Strategies

Good students have access to many learning strategies. Good students have learned when, where, and how to use each strategy to best accomplish their desired learning goals. Learn as many study and memory strategies as you can. Be willing to try new strategies that you haven't tried before. Remember that what worked before may not be what will work best now. Explore new options and continue to challenge yourself to study with greater efficiency.

3. Develop Self-Discipline

You are in a stage of development that allows you more freedom and independence than you perhaps have ever had before. Most of us look forward to this stage. However, with independence comes responsibility.

College is different from high school in many respects. One difference is the greater need to discipline yourself. The basis for the definition of discipline is "guidance" or "leading." You will find many people who are willing to help you, but you must take the initiative. You will need to lead yourself through an analysis of your own study habits, determine your strengths and your deficiencies, and seek guidance in making yourself a more effective and efficient learner! Remember the adage: If it's going to be, it's up to me!

4. Make a Commitment to Excellence

Study to become a more educated individual. Keep long-range goals in mind so you won't be tempted to study just to pass the exam! Make knowledge, accuracy, and promptness key attributes of all your assignments. Remember, you are not "just getting through college"; you are developing your self and your foundation of academic knowledge for a lifetime.

5. Recognize the Opportunities of University Life

University life offers wonderful opportunities for developing character, expanding your knowledge, and experiencing a dimension of society that will never again have quite the same composition. A significant part of becoming an effective student is knowing what resources are available and how to access them. Unfortunately, many students neglect to use the many physical and intellectual resources offered by the university. Your college years are prime time learning years. Don't miss the opportunity to take advantage of the wealth of knowledge that is at your fingertips.

Choosing Classes

Registration is a time for students to select courses needed to meet academic requirements such as majors, minors, curricula, certificates, or specific degrees. A good schedule with appropriate classes may be vital to your academic success in any one term or semester. Therefore, it is very important that you spend some time and energy planning your classes before you make final selections.

The following are some considerations that will assist you in making appropriate course selections:

1.   Seek advice from a counselor, an academic advisor, or a professor to discuss the classes that might best "fit together."

Reprinted by permission: Frank Cotham.

2. Ask other students for information about specific classes and professors. Remember that students' opinions may not accurately reflect the quality of a class. Not all students have the same learning styles nor the same learning needs. A class that was unsatisfactory for someone else may be very good for you. Thus, be sure you seek information rather than just opinions.

3. Visit the professor! Inquire about the professor's style and methodology as well as his or her attitude toward students who have learning disabilities or who need extra assistance. Ask about the reading requirements, the graded paper or project requirements, and additional out-of-class assignments. Also, find out about such things as building location, hour of class, seating arrangements, and how the grading system works. They may be significant.

4. Go to the book store and review the textbooks that are required for a particular class or section. Look at the length of the textbook and the size of the print. Evaluate the readability of the text and the quality of the organization. Look for useful reference aids such as glossaries and appendices.

5. Choose classes that are compatible with your biological clock. For example, if you are not a morning person, it may not be wise for you to take an early morning class. Try to use your best part of the day to take the classes that require the most concentration.

6. Space your classes so you will not be rushed and will have time for review before and after class. Think about organizing your classes so you won't be wasting a lot of time walking back and forth between buildings or traveling from one side of campus to the other.

2

Procrastination

"Put off Until Tomorrow What You Don't Want to Do Today!"

This is the essence of procrastination. Procrastinators live in yesterday, avoid today, and have great plans for tomorrow! Deferrers delight in such words and phrases as "later," "soon," "next week," "when I can fit it in," "after I get this done," "when I have more time," "tomorrow," and the list goes on and on. Why the delay? Why the postponement?

Many of the words used to identify procrastination relate to time; more specifically, time in the future tense. However, we know that there are only 24 hours today and there will be only 24 hours tomorrow. Time is not the real factor, but more likely a camouflage for something else.

There is really nothing unhealthy about procrastination itself. When you stop to think, the things you put off don't really exist. If they haven't been started you can't postpone them. They merely remain undone.

The concern is that procrastination uses valuable energy. It takes effort to suspend the action required to accomplish a task. Moreover, most procrastinators experience some sense of guilt and/or anxiety. Thus, procrastination brings with it an aftermath of discomfort. This is when procrastination becomes an unhealthy and dysfunctional activity.

"I wish," "I hope," "if only," and "maybe" are convenient rationales for not doing whatever it is you keep saying you're going to do. They are escape words that continue to delude you. They are words that take you out of the "now" and put you into the "folly of fairyland."

You may find yourself procrastinating on occasion or as a way of life. Regardless, it is important to take a look at some possible reasons for your behavior. Procrastination is an internal enemy of accomplishment. As you gain insight into your procrastination, you will be able to conquer this college competitor.

Psychologists have varied views on the internal causes of procrastination. The key to conquering your procrastination is to understand what makes you do what you do. Perhaps I should say, "makes you NOT do what you should do!" Let's take a look at some possible reasons why people procrastinate.

Fear, avoidance, self-doubt, self-delusion, blame, sympathy, and manipulation are common reasons for procrastination. Only you can determine if one or more of these seem to fit. Be as honest as you can be in your self-evaluation. You will need to come to grips with your motivations for procrastinating before you will be in a position to make some changes. It might also help to discuss these issues with a counselor or confidant.

Fear

Fear of the unknown, fear of success, fear of failure, fear of the difficult, and fear of the boring are all pieces of the procrastination puzzle.

1. *Fear of the Unknown.* If you are uncertain what a task may be like and you are not a big risk taker, you may put it off because it is unfamiliar. Entering the world of the unknown may require change and change is often a frightening and threatening experience.
2. *Fear of Success.* Believe it or not, you may be afraid of succeeding. This may sound strange since most of us struggle to succeed, but the fear of success is a real phenomenon. You may be afraid of the expectations and responsibilities that will result if you do succeed. Will you be able to live up to them? Was that success a fluke or will you be able to do it again?
3. *Fear of Failure.* If you begin a project, you may fail to complete it or to do it well. Failure is no fun. We all try to avoid

failure. But, remember the saying: "nothing ventured; nothing gained." Fearing failure keeps us stuck. Ask yourself, "What is the worst thing that can happen?" So you fail. You will be able to handle it. Besides, you may succeed! So, why not expect the best.

4. *Fear of the Difficult.* It's not easy to want to do things that may be difficult. You may have to work harder than you are used to working. Therefore, it is very easy to put off difficult projects.

5. *Fear of the Boring.* Sometimes you will be required to do tasks that you find boring. You don't like to do boring things so you procrastinate! It's really quite simple.

Avoidance

Procrastination allows you to avoid tasks you find unpleasant for one reason or another. Avoidance is an escape mechanism.

Perhaps you have run away from or been protected from un-pleasant experiences and are unaccustomed to the challenges that they provide.

Self-Doubt

When you put things off, you are reinforcing self-doubt. Putting something off enables you to avoid knowing whether or not you can do it. Unfortunately, lacking the confidence to tackle an unknown only serves to reinforce your self-doubt and this becomes a vicious circle.

Self-Delusion

Procrastination enables you to delude yourself that you are some-thing other than what you are. The imagination can do wonderful things to keep us from seeing our real self. If you are an onlooker rather than a participant, it is easier to become the critic and to glorify yourself at the expense of someone else. Also, by procrasti-nating, you may even find yourself mentally using others' negative performances as stepping stones to elevate yourself.

Blame

When you procrastinate, it is much easier to shift responsibility from yourself and place blame on someone or something else. For example, you can justify a poor performance by blaming it on time: "I just didn't have time to do a good job." Or, you can blame the day: "This just isn't a good day." Or, you can blame the weather: "This weather makes me tired." The excuses can go on and on and on!

Sympathy

You can feel sorry for yourself and at the same time win sympathy from others for the anxiety that you are having as a result of your procrastination. Lamenting your misfortune elicits comforting words from those around you. Procrastination has now taken the attention off of the task and placed it on you. Now, you are the cen-ter of attention.

Manipulation

Procrastination can be a means whereby you manipulate others. By putting off an activity, you might be able to persuade someone else to do your work for you or at least help you. After all, the task might now be urgent and others are more likely to come to your assistance in emergency situations.

3

Motivation

On the Road to Success

Whether you are starting or continuing on the road to success, there are a series of markers that will help you keep on the trail and have a successful journey.

1. You must believe! Believe in yourself, believe in others, and believe in the process of life. You are here for a purpose and you are the only one who can do what you have been called to do.

2. Keep an open mind! Be aware of the things that are working and the things that are not. Be willing to change the things that are not working and make them work.

3. Know when you need help and be willing to ask for it! There are many people who are very willing to assist you if they know what you need. Be specific when you ask for help.

4. Develop an attitude of gratitude! Be grateful for what you have and have been given. Be grateful for what is going to come into your life, trusting that it will be for the good.

5. Use your resources! There are many resources available to you. Use them: People, books, nature, life, experiences, events, travel—that which is seen and that which is unseen.

6. Remember that storms never last! The sun will shine again. Clouds are temporary. And, always know that behind the clouds, the sun is always shining.

7. Remember who you are and why you are here! Remind your-self what it is that you want to accomplish. Keep your eyes on that which is to be accomplished. Always look to the fu-ture; keep your chin up, your feet marching forward, and your energy directed toward your goal.

8. Balance your life. When things aren't in balance, they wob-ble. There is a wear and tear on a part of one's life force. There is a weariness that occurs when life's energies are out of harmony. Body, mind, and spirit need nurturing on a daily basis. If you neglect one, you will be in danger of draining the life energy from another. Soon you will have two that are in deficit. Balance!

9. Enjoy what you are doing. Life is short. Tomorrow is an un-known. Enjoy the day. Seize each hour that has been given to you. You are important, for no one else can do exactly what you can do or be exactly who you are.

10. Go for it! You have all the time, talent, and tools necessary to succeed. Be willing to risk. Be willing to fail. Be willing to succeed. ALL experiences in life are great teachers. If we are

© 1989, 1990, 1991, 1992 Joel Pett, Lexington Herald-Leader. Reprinted by permission.

willing, we learn great lessons from everything. We gain character and strength from all of life's events, both positive and negative. Trust the process. Trust the powers that are yours to use. Smile! Laugh! Cry! Be happy! THE VICTORY IS YOURS! YOU ARE A WINNER!

Be Willing to Try and Try and Try!

The prerequisite for mastery in most activities is the willingness to try something new and to try it over and over. More often than not you will need to try, fail, correct your errors, try again, and perhaps fail again. The key is that you keep on trying.

Success doesn't come easily for most people. To become good at something often takes lots of hard work and many attempts!

Consider the poem which speaks of the struggles of humankind, both male and female. Its message is valuable and you may need to read it often.

DON'T QUIT

When things go wrong, as they sometimes will,
When the road you're trudging seems all up hill,
When the funds are low and the debts are high,
And you want to smile, but you have to sigh,
When care is pressing you down a bit,
Rest, if you must—but don't you quit.

Life is queer with its twists and turns,
As everyone of us sometimes learns,
And many a failure turns about
When he might have won had he stuck it out;
Don't give up, though the pace seems slow—
You might succeed with another blow.

Often the goal is nearer than
It seems to a faint and faltering man,
Often the struggler has given up
When he might have captured the victor's cup.
And he learned too late, when the night slipped down,
How close he was to the golden crown.

Success is failure turned inside out—
The silver tint of the clouds of doubt—
And you never can tell how close you are,
It may be near when it seems afar;
So stick to the fight when you're hardest hit—
It's when things seem worst that you mustn't quit.

Anonymous

Some people keep going, even when they fail again and again. Consider the failures of this politician.

Failed in business	1831
Defeated for Legislature	1832
Second failure in business	1833
Suffered nervous breakdown	1836
Defeated for Speaker	1840
Defeated for Elector	1840
Defeated for Congress	1843
Defeated for Senate	1855
Defeated for Vice President	1856
Defeated for Senate	1858

If you know your United States history, you will recognize this famous politician as Abraham Lincoln, who was elected sixteenth President of the United States of America in 1860. Although he had many successes, which earned him a prominent place in history, he also had many failures. If he had given up after any one of these failures, he would have never won the highest elected office in the United States. His historical acclaim is due, in part, to the fact that he didn't quit.

Affirmations for a Positive Mental Attitude

There may be times when the pressures in your life seem overwhelming and you find yourself losing your sense of harmony and control. At times like this, get into a comfortable position, do some deep breathing, and slowly repeat the following affirmations. You may choose to play soft music in the background.

Repeat this exercise as often as necessary throughout the day
to help you re-establish your sense of feeling centered:

> I am an intelligent person.
> I am a competent and capable student.
> I continue to learn new things every day.
> My mind is filled with knowledge.
> I understand when I read and listen.
> I remember what I learn.
> I perform at a high level of achievement.
> I feel more confident every day.
> I have time to do the things I need and want to do.
> I relax my body, my mind, and my spirit.
> I get better every day.
> I am on the road of success.
> I am becoming a fantastic person.
> I am happy!
> Life holds great promise!
> The victory is mine!

Add your own personalized affirmations.

4

Goal Setting

If You Aim at Nothing, You're Sure to Hit it.

So the saying goes. Successful people have a goal; a specific dream that they desire to turn into reality. They are also motivated to bring that dream to fruition. How do they do it? What does it take to set a goal and bring it into being?

Identify Your Desires

You must desire to do better or do something differently than you are presently doing. Many students make general statements about wanting to do better in their academic studies, but that is as far as it goes. Desires must be translated into action. Therefore, once you begin to experience a desire for academic success, it is important to clarify that desire. What is it that you really want?

Clarify Your Goals

To help you clarify your desire and turn it into a goal, make a list of all the academic accomplishments that you would like to achieve. Begin by writing down every thought that comes to mind. This type of brainstorming will help you sort out specific objectives.

After you make this general list, you can begin to identify the goals that are top priority. When you zero in on your most important objectives, prioritize them. Which ones are most important to

your overall academic endeavors? Which ones can you accomplish short-term? Which ones are long-term and need a more complex plan of action?

Design a Plan of Action

After you have clarified your specific goal or goals, list the steps that it will take to achieve each goal. These steps must be specific and they should be small enough to be easily achieved on a daily basis. It is important that you can see and feel your progress so you will be encouraged and stay motivated.

Study your past record of achievement. Compare your previous record with your new goals. Learn from your past behaviors, but be challenged by your new aspirations. Think big, but be realistic. It is better to revise a goal upward than to have to reduce it drastically. However, if you set your goal too low, you won't stretch yourself.

Put Your Goals in Writing

Commit your goals and plan of action to paper. This is important since your goals will remain nebulous as long as they remain only in your head. Once you put them on paper, you make a greater commitment to those goals since they now have a physical dimension.

Sometimes it is good to share your goals. Other times it is best to keep your goals to yourself. You must decide which is best for you. Whatever your decision, write them down and put your written goals in a place where they can be seen on a daily basis. Seeing your goals often will help you to keep them a top priority.

Remain Flexible

Your goals should be specific, but not set in concrete. It is important to remain flexible and be prepared for the unexpected. Should the unexpected be an obstacle, be willing to make some mid-course corrections. Success is rarely a straight road. There are often many bumps and curves with roadblocks and detours when least expected. No person can predict the unexpected. Thus, if you make your goals for success a journey as well as a destination, you will discover that the experience with your academic studies will be more rewarding.

Be Committed

Many of us fail to reach our goals because we are not really committed to reaching them. This includes not being willing to make the sacrifices necessary to accomplish what we say we desire. Often, it is easier to blame others for our failures than to take a close look at what we did or neglected to do that could have been the determining factor.

For example, if you desire a better grade in a particular subject, you must be willing to spend more time in effective study. To do this, you may have to give up some of your co-curricular activities in order to devote more time to your studying. Too often we want to eat our cake and have it too. However, if you are truly committed to a goal, you will make the ultimate effort rather than blame your teacher for not going over the material or making the test too hard.

Expect Success

There are many who don't succeed, but few who can't. A major obstacle to success is an expectation of failure that is more powerful than an expectation of success. In his book, *See You at the Top,* Zig Zigler says that "winning is not everything, but the effort to win is." One tends to put forth more effort when there is an expectation of success. Thus, one very important ingredient in goal setting is to expect to succeed and then put forth the effort to bring that about.

If there has been a pattern of failure and disappointment in your academic endeavors, it may be that you are receptive to self-defeating behaviors. If this has been the case, you can learn how to make a more concerted effort to change your expectations. We tend to see what we look for and we tend to get what we expect. Therefore, look for that which is good and expect to succeed in accomplishing goals that you desire. Remember, it takes as much energy to think negatively as it does to think positively. Consequently, it would seem more beneficial to hold positive thoughts and expect success.

Establish Long-Term and Short-Term Goals

If you don't know where you are going, it will be hard to plan the route. A student with no purpose is like a ship without a rudder. Each one is likely to drift.

Long-range goals provide a direction and give a purpose for charting our daily course. Long-range goals serve as a buffer to help us cope with short-term frustrations. Occasionally, circumstances arise that become temporary obstacles or setbacks in the pursuit of short-term academic goals. These obstacles or setbacks can become major stumbling blocks if there are no long-term goals to stabilize your focus and direct your energy.

What would you like to achieve in the next year? The next three years? The next five years? What grade point average would you like to earn? What degree would you like to obtain? These are some excellent questions to ask yourself as you embark on the task of setting long-term goals.

Short-term goals provide the beacons that light the path to our dream. Daily objectives build character for they require dedication, determination, and discipline. Just as great cathedrals have strong foundations, it is the daily attention to one's short-term goals that support the attainment of a bigger dream. The weight lifter knows that to win top honors takes strengthening and expanding his or her muscles on a daily basis. Achieving academic excellence is no different. Studying on a daily basis will build the necessary foundations for attaining honors on your final evaluations.

Be Confident

Competence produces confidence and confidence produces competence. This is a powerful cycle. It is one that cannot fail for the more you study and become competent, the more confidence you will have in your abilities. And, the more confident you are, the more you will expect that you can be competent. Knowledge carries a lot of power and prestige; the person who possesses a genuine self-confidence is one who is frequently revered. If you are caught in this cycle, there is no way you can lose. This is a double win! Go for it! You can do it!

5

Organization

I Have to Get Organized!

I HAVE TO GET ORGANIZED! How many times have you said this to yourself? Probably, too many! So now is the time to GET ORGANIZED. Use these key principles to assist you.

1. Practice the principle of DO IT NOW! If it has to be done, it has to be done. So, you might just as well use the energy you would expend on thinking about it to go ahead and do it. Then, it will be done and you can get on to other things.
2. Learn when to say "yes" and when to say "no."
3. Discipline yourself to execute your decisions effectively.
4. Prepare for last minute interruptions by not waiting until the last minute.
5. Organize your tasks into groups so you can take care of similar things at the same time.
6. Assist your memory by placing things in a specific location where you will see them.
7. Have all your materials ready before you begin a task.
8. Keep a calendar. Organize yourself on a daily/weekly basis so you keep a balance in your life. Keeping a weekly calendar of activities will help you see at a glance if you are overbooking activities that are consuming time, but do not move you toward your goals.
9. Make a list of the things you need to do. Prioritize them. Begin with the most important first. Or, do the easiest first. Or, do the hardest first. If all the things on your list need to

"And then, of course, there's the possibility of being just the slightest bit too *organized."*
Reprinted with permission: Glen Dines

be done, then it is important to just get them done! Remember, however, that a "to do" list is usually composed of urgent items as well as non-urgent items. Don't forget your goals.

10. Think of things that have to be done and organize them in efficient time blocks. For example, if you have a library book that is due and you have to go by the library on your way to class, take the library book with you and return it.

11. Organize and execute around priorities! Decide what is urgent and important. Do those things first.

12. Learn from good role models. Many people have excellent organizational skills that are worth emulating.

Establishing Priorities

College life provides opportunities for experiencing many exciting activities. The new environment will offer cultural and educational ventures, athletic events, shopping, recreation and social activities, to name but a few. All of these things are important parts of a balanced life and will be enjoyable to experience.

However, the key is balance. If you study all the time, you will miss out on some very important social opportunities, but if you party too much you will miss out on some very important study time and may jeopardize your privilege of staying in college. So, this is the time to learn the importance of establishing priorities.

This may be the first real opportunity you have had to be on your own. You might be tempted to live it up and enjoy all the social activities that are offered. We all like to be popular and socially accepted by our peers. So, the temptation is to say yes to social opportunities that will help us feel included and well-liked. This is one of the big pitfalls.

When you have not taken the time to establish your priorities, you may find that you won't have any barometer whereby you can measure the wisdom of your decision making. Thus, a very important activity to do right now is to establish your priorities.

Make a "To Do" List

A simple procedure to help you establish priorities is to make a list of all the things you have to do or would like to do. Many people use a "to do" list to help them remember daily responsibilities. Our "to do" list is going to serve a greater purpose. So, number your paper and just start making your list. Your list might resemble the following:

1. Do laundry
2. Return library book
3. Make room and board payment
4. Pick up dry cleaning
5. Buy folders

This is an example of a typical "to do" list. It is a list of the daily tasks or maintenance activities that are necessary in order to keep your life functioning in some semblance of order.

However, in an effort to establish priorities so you can make wiser decisions about balancing your life's activities, let's amplify the "to do" list concept. Continue your list. This time be sure to include some of the things you need to do and some you would like to do, but which may be less urgent. The additions to your list may look like this:

6. Read a novel
7. Write term paper
8. Apply for student teaching
9. Study for geology exam
10. Find a part-time job
11. Go to a party
12. Plan spring vacation trip

You will need to prioritize all the things to do that are longer-term and more complex than routine daily-maintenance tasks. So, look them over carefully and think about their importance. Establishing priorities will be impacted by the purpose of the activity, the results you expect, and the deadline.

Let's work with items 6–12 as an example. I will determine that this is their order of priority:

1. Apply for student teaching
2. Find a part-time job
3. Study for geology exam
4. Plan spring vacation trip
5. Write term paper
6. Go to a party
7. Read a novel

Now that our "to do" list has been prioritized, it will be important to list each item on a separate sheet of paper with its priority sequence identified. These items will now be reclassified as projects. Since you will be frazzled trying to do more than four projects at any one time, you will need to complete one of them before you add your fifth priority to the list.

For each of your four priorities, you will need to make a list of "to dos" that will relate only to that specific item. For example, applying for student teaching has certain requirements. So you will need to list the things you need to do to accomplish this task successfully.

Now, your list might look something like this:

Apply for Student Teaching

1. Pick up forms
2. Complete forms
3. Get letter of recommendation
4. Complete 90 hours of observation
5. Turn in forms by deadline

After you have made a list of the necessary tasks that need to be completed in order to fulfill your purpose (to submit your papers on time so you will be considered for placement) and to get the desired results by the specified deadline (student teaching as scheduled so you will graduate), you will need to organize them in sequence. Here's an example.

1. **Pick up forms**
2. **Get letter of recommendation**

    a. Select individuals to ask
    b. Contact selected individuals
    c. Write letter of request

    d. Wait for letter of recommendation
    e. Write thank you note

3. Arrange for last three hours of 90-hour requirement

    a. Decide on location of observation
    b. Call to make arrangements
    c. Make observation
    d. Get signature for official documentation

4. Complete forms

    a. Make xerox copy of forms
    b. Pencil in xerox forms
    c. Type original forms

5. Compile final packet of application forms and make copies
6. Submit forms before deadline

Taking the time to prioritize your tasks and organize them in the suggested manner will help you accomplish your goals. Having specific goals and knowing what it will take to successfully complete those goals will help you make wise decisions about what other activities you have time for on any particular day or week. Goals, priorities, and deadlines must all be considered collectively as you seek to keep a healthy balance in your life and make wise choices about your use of your time.

6

Time Management

Time is one of the most interesting commodities in existence today. It is an unusual commodity that can't be seen and yet it can be measured. It can't be felt and yet it can have a profound impact on individuals and the world at large. Time is a priceless resource that can't be reused; once it is gone, it is gone. However, time is renewable in that each day you are given a new twenty-four hours to use, knowing that at the end of the day it too will be gone.

The *American College Dictionary* has over forty definitions of the word time. Time is difficult to describe. Brilliant scientists and philosophers find its definition elusive. Yet, time is something that we value, we need, and we can not live without.

Time is an equal opportunity resource. It is perhaps the only equalizer in the human realm. No matter how important, how rich, how intelligent, or what race, color, or creed you are, you will have the same amount of time in a day as everyone else. Twenty-four hours a day and 168 hours a week are yours to use—in whatever way you choose. That's the catch! How will you choose to use your time?

Time is relative. Sometimes it goes quickly and sometimes it seems to drag. At a party when you are having fun, time flies and the party ends all too soon. However, on Friday afternoons, time drags and classes may seem to be twice as long as they actually are. There are magic moments when we become so absorbed in what we are doing that hours seem like minutes, and then, there are those moments when a minute seems like an eternity. In reality, however, each minute of each day moves at the same speed. The speed of time is out of our control. What is in our control is the management of time.

Time is a gift. The management of time is a skill. Knowing how to manage time effectively gives you a chance to spend one of your most valuable resources in any way you choose. You are in charge! Do you have time? Yes! You have twenty-four hours a day. But, how much time you feel you have will depend upon your skill in using time. It will depend upon your choices, your priorities, and your ability to get the most value for each minute you spend.

There are a number of helpful time management skills proven to be effective. Take inventory of the ones that you already use and then consider adding others to your repertoire. It is very possible that learning just one or two new time management skills could be keys to your more efficient use of time. Consequently, you may increase your productivity and accomplish more of your goals and desires.

Monthly/Weekly/Daily Planning

Monthly Planning: Planning Ahead Is an Important Part of Time Management.

1. Each month, make a graphic chart of the special activities or academic requirements that are scheduled.
2. For example, write in activities such as examinations, research papers that are due, the Homecoming Dance, and weekend travel. This will help by giving you the big picture.
3. Now, you will be in a better position to program your weekly schedule to include necessary time to prepare for and accommodate these specific activities.

Weekly Scheduling: Take Time to Plan Your Week.

1. Begin by keeping track of a routine week of activities in relationship to time.

Reprinted by permission: Frank Cotham.

2. Use the Weekly Time Schedule at the end of this chapter to record all your activities. Adapt it to your individual life style. Be as specific as possible. This will help you to be accountable for the small chunks of time as well as the large chunks.

3. After you have completed a time schedule for a typical week, divide your activities into two categories. Make a list of your FIXED activities such as classes, work hours, church participation, eating, sleeping, and other regular routines. Add up the number of hours and parts of hours that you used for your FIXED activities. Subtract this figure from 168 hours to calculate the approximate number of hours left in your week for study and other FLEXIBLE activities.

4. Next, make a list of your FLEXIBLE activities such as recreation, socialization, television and movie viewing, and other activities that you may choose to do. Divide your FLEXIBLE activities into two categories: personal time and academic time. Now add up the number of hours and parts of hours used for FLEXIBLE personal activities and FLEXIBLE academic activities. You may be surprised to learn how much time you have for study!

Consider this example:

1. Fixed = 62
2. Flexible, Personal = 52
3. Flexible, Academic = 30
4. Total hours used: 62+52+30 = 144
5. Total hours available: 168–144 = 24

This means that there are still twenty-four flexible hours available for you to use. How about adding a few more hours to your study schedule?

Daily Priorities: Take Time to Plan Your Day!

1. Each day fill out a "to do" list such as the Daily Planning Guide at the end of this chapter. List the things that are necessary for you to accomplish.

2. Prioritize your list.

3. Arrange your list according to academic and personal priorities.

4. Organize your list into groups. For example, assume that you have to do your laundry today. Let's also assume that you have to memorize twenty words for a vocabulary test. These may be good activities to group together in that you can memorize your words while you are waiting for your laundry.

5. Cross off each item as it is completed. This will give you a feeling of accomplishment as you will readily be able to see your progress.

6. Work hard to complete your list each day. If you do not complete a task on today's list, place it as a priority on tomorrow's list.

7. Each night before you go to bed, make a tentative list of the things that you have to do the next day. This will give you a head start in organizing your upcoming day.

Study Time

1. A good general principle to follow is to spend at least two hours of study time for every hour you spend in class. If you spend fifteen hours in class, plan to spend a minimum of thirty hours in effective study. Remember that, at this point in time, school is your job and if you were employed you would be responsible for spending time carrying out your responsibilities.

2. Organize your time in a series of short sessions. For example, it is better to spend two two-hour sessions than spend four straight hours in study. If you should decide to spend four straight hours studying, be sure to take frequent breaks.

3. Study in short sessions over longer periods of time. Consider this illustration. If you can only study for five hours during a week, it might be best to study an hour a day for each of the five days.

4. Set a goal for the amount of time you will spend in concentrated study time. You might consider setting a timer for twenty to forty minutes. Then, make it a goal to focus on your study for that length of time. When the timer rings, give yourself a little break and return for another segment of studying.

Biological-Clock Studying

Determine the time of the day you study with the greatest benefit. There seems to be a time of the day when people are most alert and a time when they are less sharp.

Pay attention to your sleep patterns, times during the day when you seem to have the most energy, and times when you seem to be a little slow.

1. Take your hardest classes during your most alert hours, if you have a choice.

2. Study during your alert hours.

3. Do routine tasks and recreational activities when your mental abilities are least effective.

Use the Weekly Subject Planner form at the end of this chapter to record examinations and key assignments. Plan your most effec-

Reprinted by permission: Tribune Media Services.

tive and available study times. You won't be sorry you spent the time doing this activity. The payoff will be tremendous.

Time Management Tips

The following time tips and suggestions will help you use your time more effectively.

1. Wait Time

When you have to wait, use your time effectively. Carry a card pack with you at all times so you can study your notes or memorize specific information.

2. Commute Time

Commute time can be thought of as time used to get from one place to another. We are often unaware of the amount of time we spend in transit. Often, commuting is thought of in relationship to automobiles or public transportation such as riding the bus or taking the subway. However, don't forget how much time you use in walking, riding your bicycle, or using other forms of transportation.

Minutes make hours and hours add up. So, be creative and make good use of your commute time. Here are some suggestions to stimulate your thinking.

1. Commute time is an excellent opportunity to listen to tapes on topics related to your personal growth or academic studies.
2. Commute time can also be used for organizing and planning your day.
3. If someone else is driving, commute time is also a good time to use your card pack for memorizing specified information.
4. Thinking about or conceptualizing ideas for assigned projects or papers can be done while you are in transit.
5. Relaxation and contemplation are important aspects of effective learning. Remember, commute time can also be reserved for this kind of activity.

3. Deadlines

Set a deadline for each task and do your best to stick to it. A project doesn't become an action program until you set a deadline and begin working toward it.

You might also consider setting intermediate deadlines, which could be several weeks, a week, or at least a few days ahead of the actual deadline established by your teacher. This will help you get going and keep you working at a steady pace. Thus, a frantic burst of energy will not be needed at the last minute and you may eliminate a crisis should something unexpected happen to alter your time schedule.

Remember Parkinson's Law: "Work expands to fill the time available for its contemplation."

4. Decision Making

Some decisions require lots of time for deliberation and should not be made hastily. However, many decisions are minor day-to-day decisions and should be made as quickly as possible. If you postpone action until all objections are overcome, you may waste a lot of time. Make your decision, move into action, and modify as necessary.

5. Interruptions

Organize your study time so you minimize interruptions. One of the benefits of concentrated activity is that you decrease the amount of time it takes to warm up for one activity and shift gears for another one. Eliminate unnecessary distractions by taking care of potential interruptions before you begin studying.

6. Meetings

If your school activities require participation in meetings, here are some important points to remember:

1. Begin and end meetings on time.
2. Stick to the agenda.
3. Try to reach some kind of decision on the designated purpose of the meeting.
4. At the end of the meeting, restate the decisions reached and any assignments given to individual members.

7. Say "No"

Be willing to say no to every request that does not contribute to the achievement of your goals. According to Bliss, "of all the time saving techniques ever developed, perhaps the most effective is the frequent use of the word no" (Bliss 1976, p. 100). Peer pressure is real and there will be many demands for your time, particularly if you are talented and/or popular. Keep your goals in mind and don't waste time participating in nonproductive activities.

8. Procrastination

Although procrastination was covered in Chapter 2, no discussion of time management would be complete without bringing it to your attention once again. Procrastination eats time!

Usually when you procrastinate the task mysteriously multiplies and takes far more time than it would have taken if done earlier. Even if the physical task takes no longer, remember that you have spent extra time thinking about the fact that you have something to do that you have not done.

Perhaps the most valuable result of all education is the ability to make yourself do the thing you have to do when it ought to be done, whether you like it or not; it is the first lesson that ought to be learned; and however early a man's training begins, it is probably the last lesson that he learns thoroughly

— Thomas Huxley

Time-Eating Temptations

College has lots of deadlines! Thus, time is limited. So, it is important not to waste time. It goes quickly, particularly if you yield to
"time-eating" temptations.

Use the following checklist to determine if you are losing valuable time. Remember that none of these activities are inherently
negative. However, if they consume too much time and, thus, limit
your study activities, you may need to reevaluate your academic
goals and work to bring a better balance to your college life.

1. Talking on the telephone
2. Sleeping
3. Listening to radio
4. Watching television
5. "Partying"
6. Daydreaming
7. Playing games/doing hobbies
8. Procrastinating/worrying
9. Goofing off
10. Visiting
11. Hanging out in the local gathering place
12. Playing recreational sports
13. Going home on weekends
14. Reading material not related to your goals
15. _____

Add personalized statements that are not reflected on the list.

Weekly Time Schedule

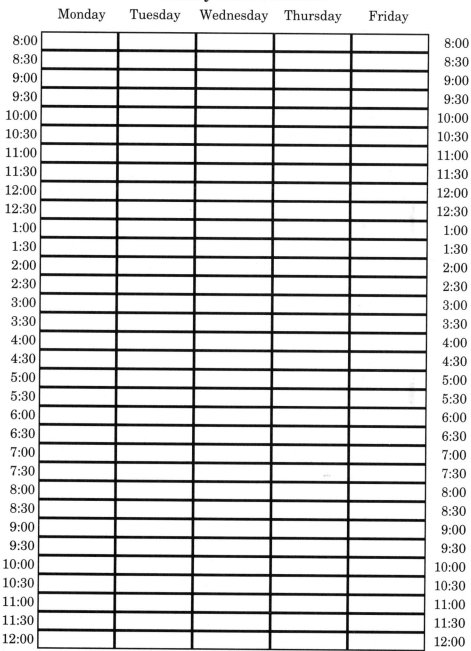

	Monday	Tuesday	Wednesday	Thursday	Friday	
8:00						8:00
8:30						8:30
9:00						9:00
9:30						9:30
10:00						10:00
10:30						10:30
11:00						11:00
11:30						11:30
12:00						12:00
12:30						12:30
1:00						1:00
1:30						1:30
2:00						2:00
2:30						2:30
3:00						3:00
3:30						3:30
4:00						4:00
4:30						4:30
5:00						5:00
5:30						5:30
6:00						6:00
6:30						6:30
7:00						7:00
7:30						7:30
8:00						8:00
8:30						8:30
9:00						9:00
9:30						9:30
10:00						10:00
10:30						10:30
11:00						11:00
11:30						11:30
12:00						12:00

Daily Planning Guide

To Do List

1. _____
2. _____
3. _____
4. _____
5. _____
6. _____

Today's Priorities

1. _____
2. _____
3. _____
4. _____
5. _____
6. _____

Tomorrow's Plans

1. _____
2. _____
3. _____
4. _____
5. _____
6. _____

Weekly Subject Planner

Name _____

Week Date _____

Subjects	Monday	Tuesday	Wednesday	Thursday	Friday

Saturday

Sunday

Projects Due:

Examinations:

Deadlines

Deadlines are a necessary part of achievement! Since college is an achievement-oriented system, there will be deadlines. If you want some form of evaluation for the work that you have produced, then there must come a time when your work needs to be finished and submitted for evaluation.

You have already developed habits and strategies for coping with deadlines. These habits have been developing over a long period of time. So, it would probably be wise to take a serious look at your habits—the good ones and the bad ones.

Spend a few moments thinking about these questions and then answer them as honestly as you can.

1. What are my feelings about deadlines?
2. How do I prepare to meet deadlines?

Reprinted by permission: Tribune Media Services.

What are your feelings about deadlines? These might have been some of the thoughts that raced through your mind:

Deadlines stink!
Deadlines can be ignored.
Deadlines can be stretched.
Deadlines are made to be broken.
Deadlines are insignificant.
Deadlines are scary.
Deadlines cause anxiety.
Deadlines are made to be kept.
Deadlines are important.

Some of the habits that you have developed are directly related to your feelings about deadlines. If you think they are insignificant and can be ignored or stretched, then you may not work very hard to meet them. If, on the other hand, you think they are important and should be honored, then you will try to keep them.

In college, it will be important to honor deadlines. Some professors will listen to your procrastinations and pleas for mercy. However, some professors will lower grades for lateness and others will simply not accept late work. So, if you don't honor deadlines, you may put your grades in jeopardy.

Let's assume you want to honor all deadlines. HOW WILL YOU DO IT? More importantly, how will you do it without experiencing the anxiety of a last minute frenzy or pulling an all-nighter?

Here is a three-step plan that is functional for coping with deadlines:

1. *Deadlines.* Record a deadline on your master calendar just as soon as you are notified of it.
2. *Pre-Deadlines.* Plan to have your project done a week, or at least a few days, ahead of the designated deadline.
3. *Stepping-Stone Deadlines.* Divide your project or paper into a series of stepping stones. Then, create a milestone deadline for each of these steps. Space these milestone deadlines reasonably within the structure of your schedule.

In a sense, you are starting at the end and working backward toward the beginning. Now that you have created backward deadlines, you can work forward on your journey toward completing your goal ON TIME!

Use the following illustration to help you get a better grasp of the way the three-step deadline plan works.

PROBLEM: WRITING A PAPER
DEADLINE: MARCH 20
PRE-DEADLINE: MARCH 13
STEPPING-STONE DEADLINES:

Task	*Time Guide*	
1. Choose a topic	JAN	20
2. Brainstorm key words for topic	JAN	24
3. Formulate questions to guide research	FEB	1
4. Begin topical outline	FEB	7
5. Collect information	FEB	13
6. Make bibliography cards	FEB	27
7. Write a first draft	MAR	2
8. Seek assistance for improvements	MAR	7
9. Write the final document	MAR	13
10. Submit the paper	MAR	20

By dividing larger tasks into smaller ones, you will be able to organize your time and capitalize on your creativity more effectively. Always remember to create some cushion zones in case you become ill or have some other type of emergency.

This deadline plan works very well. However, like any plan, it only works if you work it.

8

Learning Styles

How Do You Learn?

The human brain's two hemispheres have different but overlapping skills or ways of processing information. You most likely have a tendency to process information in a preferred manner even though you realize that both sides of the brain are working in harmony. Likewise, remember that your brain will need to shift from hemisphere to hemisphere depending upon the skills needed at any specific time in order to accomplish a particular task.

The following categories of some basic functions will give you an idea of hemispheric specialization.

LEFT	*RIGHT*
Analytical	Intuitive
Linear	Holistic
Explicit	Spontaneous
Sequential	Diffused
Verbal	Nonverbal
Concrete	Symbolic
Rational	Emotional
Goal-oriented	Artistic
Auditory	Visual
Logical	Creative
Thinking	Physical

Using principles of right and left hemispheric dominance, let's look at where some of the academic skills might be processed.

LEFT	*RIGHT*
Auditory/Listening	Pictures
Phonics	Sight Words
Handwriting	Shapes and Patterns
Talking/Reciting	Doing/Touching/Moving
Sequences	Creativity
Language	Art/Music
Time Oriented	Not Time Oriented
Focuses	Scans
Repetition/Drill	Rhythm/Movement
Details	Big Picture
Blends together	Breaks apart
Two-dimensional	Three-dimensional

For an interesting and understandable discussion of hemispheric activity, read *Whole Brain Thinking* by Jacquelyn Wonder and Priscilla Donovan, 1984 or *Is The Left Brain Always Right* by Clare Cherry, Douglas Godwin, and Jesse Staples, 1989.

Preferred Learning Style Profile

Instructions: Place a check beside the statements that apply to you. See if you have a strong preference for one of the styles presented. If you have a strong preference for a particular style, emphasize that style when you study. For example, if you have a preference for the visual mode, draw pictures to depict information, use charts, and try to watch videos to gain an understanding of the content. Determine if you have a secondary preference as it may not always be possible to use your primary preference.

Common Characteristics

I. Visual

_____   like visual presentations
_____   have strong sense of color/patterns
_____   have difficulty with auditory directions

_____ may have artistic ability
_____ distracted by sound

II. Auditory
_____ prefer to listen to information
_____ have difficulty with reading
_____ favor verbal directions
_____ remember words that have been spoken
_____ store spoken words like a recording

III. Haptic
_____ have difficulty sitting still
_____ prefer hands-on activities
_____ learn better with physical activity
_____ may have athletic ability
_____ remember best by writing/drawing/doing

Study Characteristics Profile

Becoming an excellent student requires that you recognize your study characteristics and preferences. The following profile is not all-inclusive. However, it will give you a good overview of the characteristics related to your style of functioning. This, in turn, will alert you to how and when you need to study and what characteristics you may need to modify in order to become a more effective student.

Review the following study preference profile. Determine your basic or primary preferences and styles. Highlight or circle those that relate to you. Build on your strong points and work to improve areas that are weak.

1. Day Person   Night Person
2. Silence   Sound
            Music   Television   Radio
3. Auditory   Visual   Kinesthetic/Tactile   Multisensory
4. Short Term Study   Long Term Study   Cramming
5. Self Study   Partner Study   Group Study
6. Organized   Moderately Organized   Disorganized
7. Attentive   Mind Wanders   Can't Concentrate
8. Work Well Under Pressure   Buckle Under Pressure
9. Plan Ahead   Meet Deadlines   Miss Deadlines
10. Self-Starter   Other-Motivated   Unmotivated
11. Calm   Active   Overactive   Hyperactive
12. Good Memory   Weak Memory   Poor Memory
13. Good Management Skills   Weak Management Skills
14. Sleep Needs: 6 hours 7 hours 8 hours 9 hours 10 hours
15. Clear Desk   Moderately Clear Desk   Cluttered Desk
16. Bright Lights   Medium Lights   Dim Lights
17. Bright Colors   Medium Colors   Dull Colors
18. Formal Seating   Informal Seating

List other characteristics that you think are significant.

9

Study Strategies

Strategies for Studying Text

Information Explosion Era

Like it or not, we live in an age of information explosion and each year an extraordinary amount of information and technical knowledge becomes available. Textbooks are getting bigger and bigger. Some classes require that more than one text be read and studied. Thus, the amount of information a student must read and comprehend is phenomenal!

Although there are many study strategies that can be used, you will find the following suggestions to be very valuable.

1. Get Acquainted with Your Book

    a. Look through your book, cover to cover.
    b. Read the Table of Contents.
    c. Review the Preface so you will better understand the purpose of the text.
    d. Peruse the content, chapter by chapter.
    e. Evaluate the organization of the text.
    f. Take note of the typographical aids such as special headings, graphs, charts, pictures, and italicized passages.
    g. Notice the aids at the end of the book. Look at the Glossary, the Index, the Appendices, and the Bibliography.

"IF YOU WILL REMEMBER, BOBBY, I URGED YOU TO STUDY HARDER!"

Reprinted by permission: Frank Gotham.

2. Paper Clip Your Chapters

a. Place a paper clip on the first page of each chapter. This practice will help you with your organization and will save time as you are looking for items within a specific chapter. Also, it will give you a psychological edge in that chapters will seem more manageable than the whole text.

3. Read the Chapter Summary

a. Read the chapter summary before you read the content of the chapter.

b. Think about what you already know in relationship to the content.

c. Think about what you would like to find out as you read the chapter.

4. Use the SQ3R Method

a. Use the SQ3R study formula (Survey, Question, Read, Recite, Review).

b. Apply this adaptation of SQ3R: Survey, Summary, Question, Read, Write, Recite, and Review.

    1. Survey the chapter or section.
    2. Read the summary.
    3. Ask appropriate questions.
    4. Read the chapter or section.
    5. Write a summary of what you read.
    6. Recite the information, audibly if possible.
    7. Review your work.

5. Read a Section and Write a Summary

a. Read a section of your text and then write a summary of the important ideas.

b. Write the information in your own words, but don't be too wordy.

c. Personalize the information so it is meaningful to you.

6. Carry on a Conversation with Your Book

"Talk to your book as your book talks to you."

a. Highlight the main ideas. A pale yellow highlighter is suggested.

b. Circle key words within the highlighted passages.

c. Number sequences or words in a list.

d. Write important points and key words in the margins.

e. Write notes of agreement and disagreement in response to the content.

f. Think of the book as a letter rather than a text. Read it expecting to react to it.

g. Record questions you would like to ask the author.

7. Draw Pictures or Designs of the Key Ideas

a. Use kinesthetic and visual methods to assist memorizing information.

b. Remember, a picture is worth a thousand words.

8. Dramatize the Information

a. Dramatize the information.

b. Speak the information aloud.

c. Give it personal meaning and add emotion to make it more memorable.

9. Pretend You Are the Expert

a. Enter the study situation with confidence and determination.

b. Pretend you are the expert and that you are reading and making notes for your world famous lecture.

c. Think about or prepare a lesson plan that you would use if you were the teacher.

10. Search for Information on the Big Six

a. Look for information that answers the questions WHO? WHAT? HOW? WHY? WHEN? and WHERE?

11. Teach the Information to Another

a. The best way to learn is to teach others.

b. Teaching the material gives you a chance to check out how well you know the information.

12. Focus on Structural Organizers

a. *Generalization.* Usually the main idea is presented along with the supporting details.

b. *Sequence.* The material is listed according to some sequence such as time, order, or significance.

c. *Cause and Effect.* The author gives the cause and the possible effect or the effect followed by the cause.

d. *Comparison and Contrast.* One item is compared or contrasted with another item. They may be related or unrelated.

e. *Question and Answer.* The author asks a question and gives a suggested answer.

f. *Enumeration.* Items of importance are simply placed in lists. The lists may or may not be numbered.

13. Read the Text Aloud

a. Reading is a visual process. Therefore, if you read aloud you will be using the auditory channel as well as the visual mode for receiving input.

b. You should note that reading aloud will likely take more time since you can see faster than you can speak.

14. Predict Possible Test Questions

a. Anticipate test questions and study with those questions in mind.

b. Put an asterisk in the margin by the information that you predict will be on the examination.

15. Conduct Pre-Reading Activities

a. Define a purpose for reading.

b. Activate your prior knowledge by thinking about what you already know about the topic to be read.

c. Look up unknown vocabulary before you begin reading.

d. Be familiar with the author's plan of organization.

e. Organize your study area and have all necessary study tools available.

SQ3R: Study Strategy

SQ3R is a systematic approach to studying which was introduced by Robinson in 1941. SQ3R is actually a collection of study techniques compiled into a study formula which has proved to be very valuable (Robinson 1941). This study approach works best with expository texts that use headings and subheadings. The initials of the study strategy stand for:

1. Survey
2. Question
3. Read
4. Recite
5. Review

SQ3R has had a number of adaptations through the years. I suggest that students expand it to SSQ3RW. These initials stand for Summary, Survey, Question, Read, Recite, Review, and Write.

When beginning your study of a chapter, I suggest that you read the SUMMARY first.

1. Create a mind-set for the passage.
2. Think about what you already know.
3. Relate the content to yourself—personalize it.
4. Imagine yourself in the situation.
5. Visualize yourself as an EXPERT of the content.

Now, use these explanatory steps for understanding the SQ3R study strategy.

1. Survey

1. Look through the total chapter or passage.
2. Get a broad overview and a feeling for the content.

2. Question

1. Formulate questions using headings to guide you.
2. Read to find the answers to these and other questions.

3. Read

1. Read to comprehend the content and to find the answers to your questions.
2. Use metacognitive monitoring. Think about your thinking process.

4. Recite

1. Answer the questions you created at the beginning.
2. Paraphrase the passage using your own words.
3. Recite and write down the key ideas.

5. Review

1. Select appropriate memory and recall strategies.
2. Check your memory for the main points.

After reading the SUMMARY and using SQ3R, I suggest you WRITE! Use the following key points to guide you.

1. Record the key words in the passage.
2. Read and highlight important information.
3. Circle, with a pencil, key words within the highlighted areas.
4. Write key ideas and terms in the margins.
5. Make written notes and number your key ideas as you would a list.

You may need to practice this strategy for a period of weeks before it becomes internalized. However, your persistence will pay off as this strategy works!

The Inverted Study Triangle

For those of you who would benefit from seeing how to study your text, use the following inverted study triangle to help you visualize the process.

1. The widest part, or base, of the triangle, which is now at the top, represents all the words of the text that you will be reading.
2. The section below that represents all the words and phrases that you will be highlighting.
3. The section below that represents the words that you will be circling or underlining with a pencil. These may be independent of or within the already highlighted parts.
4. The bottom section, or tip of the triangle, represents the memorizing portion of your work. At this point, you will create mnemonics, or memory techniques, to help you store key information.
5. To review your understanding of what you have just read, start from the tip of the triangle and work your way back up to the

base. In other words, using your mnemonics, see if you can (1) recall key words, (2) remember important points, and (3) put an understanding of the text into your own words. This process creates a domino effect. One idea triggers another, which triggers another, which triggers another! Congratulations! You have it! Using this strategy makes test taking much easier as the information is "packaged" in a manner that lends itself to retrieval.

A Study Guide for Studying

The following are suggested as guidelines to monitor your studying and help you develop strategies for optimal learning.

1. I read the assigned text before it is presented in class.
2. I have evaluated my own study style and use that information to study effectively.
3. I am aware of how memory works and use metamemory strategies to monitor my own learning.
4. I use time management techniques to evaluate the use of my time.
5. I am aware of my daily biological clock and study my toughest content during the best times.
6. I recognize the relationship between the time spent on the task and learning.
7. I study for long range retention, not just to pass the exam!
8. I read, study, and review on a daily basis rather than focusing on deadlines.
9. I use multisensory approaches for learning and retention.
10. I am wise in the application of memory techniques such as association, linking, mnemonics, acronyms, peg systems, story memory, picture memory, muscle memory, and finger memory as I study cognitive information.
11. I set goals and establish the steps that will get me to those goals.
12. I personalize the information and make it meaningful to me and my situation.
13. I carry on a conversation with the author so I become an active participant rather than a passive reader.

14. I use SQ3R or other effective study formulas.
15. I am aware of the importance of vocabulary development and have a daily/weekly plan to increase my word knowledge.
16. I recognize the role of attitude in learning and constantly evaluate my attitude as I approach each situation.
17. I am organized and plan ahead so I have plenty of time to think and process information.
18. I take notes as I read my text. I read a section and write a summary of the main ideas and supporting details.
19. I review and relate class notes to my text and text notes immediately after class.
20. I believe that I am a capable individual and that I am accountable for my own learning. I evaluate myself before I blame others. I search for solutions and take the responsibility for doing what needs to be done in order to accomplish my goals. My teachers will always recognize me as an outstanding student in body, mind, and spirit!

10

Vocabulary

Vocabulary Development

Words, Words, Words!

There is wonder in words. Words contain the fiber of meaning for reading, writing, listening, and speaking. They are at the very core of communication. How often have you heard someone say, "I know what I want to say, but I don't know the words to say it."

Importance of Vocabulary Development

The importance of vocabulary development should not be underestimated. It is crucial. The poverty of some students' language is appalling considering the number of words that are accessible on a daily basis.

Reprinted with special permission of King Features Syndicate.

Think of the number of students who are prisoners of ignorance because much of the English language is foreign to them. This ignorance is not due to the fact that students cannot decode, or pronounce, the words. Rather it is because they cannot encode them.

According to Shepherd, "there are more than 500,000 words in the English language, but it is estimated that average well-educated Americans make practical use of only about 30,000 of these words. Thus, as you pursue your college study, you must expect that any one of more than 470,000 words that are unfamiliar to you may suddenly appear in the materials you read" (Shepherd 1981, p.47).

Vocabulary and Comprehension

Unfamiliar concepts coded into unknown words in a communication represent a chasm students cannot cross without assistance. That assistance comes from a greater knowledge of vocabulary. A strong vocabulary is your key to improved comprehension, success in studying, and a more challenging career. You are also likely to find greater self-confidence in your communication with others as your vocabulary increases.

A knowledge of words and what words mean is among the most important building blocks for intellectual functioning. Vocabulary is especially critical to comprehension and those who have acquired an extensive vocabulary are indeed fortunate.

Vocabulary Development

Vocabulary development has both horizontal and vertical perspectives. Your vocabulary bank is expanded vertically by regularly adding new words. It is increased horizontally by learning new meanings for old words.

Receptive and Expressive Vocabulary

You may think of yourself as having only one vocabulary, but you actually have two. You have a receptive vocabulary and an expressive vocabulary. The words that you know when you read or listen compose your receptive vocabulary. The words that you know when you speak or write compose your expressive vocabulary.

Your receptive vocabulary is your basic vocabulary and it is usually much larger than your expressive vocabulary. Even then, it is often limited. Shepherd states that "if you have a receptive vocabulary of 14,000 words, the chances are that in 80 percent of what you write you rely on a vocabulary of fewer than 3,000 words and that in 95 percent of what you say you use a vocabulary of fewer than 1,000 words" (Shepherd 1987, p. 3). Therefore, a primary goal of vocabulary development is to increase the size and utilization of your receptive vocabulary.

Seeking Meaning to Unknown Words

Sometimes you hear or read a word you don't know. When this happens there are several things you can do to discover its meaning: (1) You can use context clues, since often the surrounding words or ideas will provide meaning or clues to meaning; (2) You can ask someone who knows the meaning of the word; (3) You can determine what the word means by knowing the base word and its word parts; (4) You can look the word up in the dictionary.

Dictionary

The dictionary is one of the most valuable tools you will ever possess. Unfortunately, it is often used as the last resort and is frequently undervalued. The dictionary gives the pronunciation of a word, lists many different meanings, and identifies the part of speech for each specified word. Its value is immeasurable.

Thesaurus

The thesaurus is a book of synonyms for words. In many thesauruses there also are references to antonyms. Strictly speaking, synonyms are words that are different in form but are identical in meaning. However, absolute synonyms are rare. Although similar in meaning or denotation, many synonyms have different connotations or interpretations. Also, linguistic sources and usages may differ.

Vocabulary Enhancement

Acquiring a good vocabulary is a lifelong process. First, it is important that you know how to increase your vocabulary. Next, it is crucial that you do it and DO IT NOW! Successful students develop an interest in words. This interest should lead you to an enthusiasm and even a passion for language and its usage.

PEANUTS reprinted by permission of UFS, Inc.

Now that you know the importance of vocabulary, how do you go about enhancing your vocabulary? Although there are a number of ways, a few of the most fundamental ones will be presented for your consideration and application.

1. Vocabulary Notebook

Start a little notebook for vocabulary development. Let this become your developmental dictionary for receptive and expressive vocabulary.

1. Keep your vocabulary notebook handy.
2. When you see or hear a new word, write it down. You may not know how to spell it correctly, but you can always spell it phonetically—the way it sounds.
3. Look up the word in the dictionary and highlight it.
4. Talk about it. Ask others if they have heard it and if they know what it means.
5. Put the word on a 3" x 5" index card and place it in a location that is very visible.
6. Think about the word.
7. Use the word often.

2. Vocabulary Card Pack

Start a card pack of vocabulary words.

Front Side of Card:

1. Print the word in the center of the card.
2. Identify the pronunciation underneath the word using diacritical marks.

Back Side of Card:

1. Print the word on the top of the card.
2. Record the part of speech.
3. Write the meaning of the word.
4. Use the word in a sentence.

When you want to test yourself on your new vocabulary words, use the front side of the card. When you want to learn the word or check you knowledge, use the back side. Thus, your card pack can be used both for teaching and testing.

Carry your card pack with you throughout the day. When you have a few moments of wait time, you can expand and rehearse your vocabulary.

See how big you can get your word card pack. Enjoy the fact that you are bringing about the enhancement of your vocabulary!

3. Highlight Your Dictionary

Purchase a dictionary that you can make marks in. When you look up a new word, highlight it with a yellow highlighter. Every time you are using your dictionary, your eyes will be drawn to the highlighted words. This type of focus will assist you in rehearsing your new vocabulary. Both continual and intermittent repetition are important aspects of learning.

4. Write Key Words in Your Dictionary

Use the blank pages of your dictionary to write down new words that you look up that you want to remember. This will make your dictionary more personalized and add to its value. Also, by writing the word, you are utilizing the kinesthetic aspect of memory. Looking at this specific portion of your dictionary will remind you of words that you are working on to remember. Also, by recording your new words, you will be encouraged by seeing a visual record of your progress.

5. Note Multiple Meanings of Words

As many as one-third of commonly used words have multiple meanings (Devine 1987, p. 137). Such polysemous words create difficulties in comprehension. Make a list of polysemous words and record their various meanings. Use this list to enhance your vocabulary horizontally. It is important to pay particular attention to figures of speech, idioms, and the like.

6. Link Unfamiliar Words to Existing Knowledge

Learn how to use context and meanings of word parts to make inferences about unknown words. For example, let's say you are reading a science passage and you encounter the word carnivorous. You do not know the meaning of the word carnivorous, but you know the meaning of the word herbivorous. By using the content of the rest of the passage and the words that you already know, you will be in a good position to determine the meaning of the unknown word.

7. Semantic Maps

Make semantic maps in order to see a new word in a greater perspective. Begin by writing the key word in the center of your paper. Draw a circle around the key word and attach lines extending outward. List words on the end of each line that relate to the key word.

8. Feature Analysis Charts

Make a chart of the characteristics of a word's meaning. Demonstrate the features of a new word by comparing it, and contrasting it, to other members of its general class. By analyzing shared and unique features, you will add depth to your understanding.

9. Whole Word Vocabulary Acquisition

Pick a new word and practice its meaning and usage by using the whole-word approach. Choose words that are interesting and fun to say. Words that have an enjoyable rhythm and sound are frequently easier to remember. Also, choose words that are your style and that you anticipate being able to use frequently (See Figure 10–1 in this chapter).

10. Building Word Power Through Structural Analysis

One of the significant and most powerful ways to build a meaningful vocabulary is by developing knowledge of the structural aspects of words. In English, as in other languages, new words often are developed by combining old words, or word parts, with affixes or existing words. Thus, once you know the meaning of a root word or word part, you can use that knowledge and transfer it to other words that you don't know. Many students are not aware of this gold mine of knowledge.

Not all word parts have meaning in and of themselves. However, many of them do and these are the ones on which you should concentrate (See Fig. 10–2, 10–3, and 10–4 in this section).

11. A Postscript

Post = after; Script = to write. Never make the mistake of saying, "I don't need to know that word!" Words carry power. Your knowledge of words empowers you to move to higher levels of achievement.

It would be wise for you to spend time studying the meaning-based morphemes that make up thousands of English words. Knowledge of Latin-based prefixes, roots, and suffixes, as well as Greek-combining forms, will enhance your vocabulary and make spelling much easier. With a little effort you will be reading, spelling, and knowing the meaning of words such as these: spectroheliograph, ophthalmoscope and pneumonoultramicroscopicsilicovolcanoconiosis!

The Joy of Using a Dictionary

Unfortunately, most students have not learned the joy of using a dictionary. To many, the dictionary is to be avoided. Often, the dictionary is the last resort when the meaning of a word is required and you cannot find it in the glossary and no one else knows its meaning either.

Become Friends with the Dictionary

Becoming friends with the dictionary is one of the wisest behaviors you can develop as you strive to be successful in college. Learning to enjoy the dictionary does not have to be a long or difficult process. Actually, it can be quite simple and most valuable.

Use an Unabridged Dictionary

A large unabridged dictionary can be found in the library. This is a wonderful resource for it contains more words and provides more complete information on each word listed. Also, a history, or etymology, of each word is presented. This information is valuable in that it often assists in understanding the meaning of a particular word.

Purchase a Dictionary

Begin by purchasing a paperback dictionary that is not too elaborate. It should be medium in size and be extensive enough for the college level. Be sure the print is as large as possible and easy to read. It helps if the paper will tolerate the ink of a highlighter without bleeding through the page.

1. Paperback dictionary
2. Medium in size
3. Large print
4. Good quality paper

Use this dictionary as your lap dictionary. Keep it close by. Make this dictionary your companion dictionary and interact with it freely and often. If you store it on a shelf, be sure you have easy access to it. You may want to carry it in your bookbag so you will have it with you throughout the day.

Highlight the Word

When you look up a word in your dictionary, highlight the word. This technique will make the word stand out on the page. Every time that you look up another word on this page, or pass this page as you are looking up another word in the dictionary, you will notice the words that you have highlighted. Your eyes will automatically focus on these words and this will become a reinforcement for learning them. By seeing them over and over, you will be setting the stage for learning, as repetition will enhance memory.

Create Your Own Word Dictionary

If there is a page in the back, or front, of the dictionary that is relatively free of print, use this page to create your own word dictionary. When you look up a word and you know that you would like to add it to your vocabulary, write it on the designated page. Record the word and a one- or two-word definition. This will provide just enough information to stimulate your memory and will not use too much space.

This technique is also valuable for helping you with spelling. For example, you may remember the word and its meaning, but you may be uncertain as to how to spell it. If you know that it is recorded on your dictionary page, you will be able to find it more quickly. This quicker way of finding a word will encourage you to use it more frequently and, thus, you will be more apt to incorporate it into your vocabulary.

Construct a Word File

Write down words with which you are unfamiliar. Use a separate 3" x 5" index card for each word. Take the time to record the sentence or sentence part in which you found the word. Later on, you can look up the word and record its definition.

This is a terrific way to build your vocabulary, with little effort. Your card file will also serve as an efficient way to review for your examinations, as many vocabulary words will be used in the text of the exam questions or in the options for the answers.

Note: An excellent reference for developing word meaning is *Instant Vocabulary* by Ida Ehrlich and published by Pocket Books, New York.

FIGURE 10–1   Vocabulary Development Word List

1.	egghead	21.	geoducks
2.	oxymoron	22.	quahogs
3.	bogus	23.	abecedarian
4.	cogitate	24.	palindrome
5.	mnemonic	25.	dubious
6.	insouciant	26.	palpitate
7.	rapscallion	27.	spelunker
8.	prodigious	28.	loquacious
9.	pugnacious	29.	alliteration
10.	opulent	30.	xenophobia
11.	hobbledehoy	31.	pauper
12.	gobbledygook	32.	etymology
13.	triskaidekaphobia	33.	belligerent
14.	onomatopoeia	34.	stoic
15.	googol	35.	nefarious
16.	pungent	36.	lexicon
17.	pachyderm	37.	garb
18.	bodacious	38.	eclectic
19.	juxtaposition	39.	deportment
20.	pejorative	40.	agile

FIGURE 10–2   Morphology of Vocabulary Words

1.	lexicon = dictionary	lexi = words
2.	velocipede = bicycle	veloci = speed ped = foot
3.	dyslexia = dysfunction with words	dys = dysfunction lexi = words
4.	polysemous = many meanings	poly = many semantic = meanings
5.	quinquagenarian = of, or related to, the fifties	quin = five gen = kind of ian = relating to

6. triskaidekaphobia =   tri = three
    fear of thirteen   deka = ten
                                   phobia = fear of

7. hemidemisemiquaver =   hemi = half
    a 64th note   demi = half
                                   semi = half
                                   quaver = eighth note

8. intellectual =   intellectu = knowledge
    having knowledge   al = relating to

FIGURE 10–3   Knowledge of Morphemes Aids Vocabulary Development

1. auto = self   automobile, autograph, automatic
2. graph = to write   telegraph, graphology, phonograph
3. mono = one   monocle, monocycle, monotony
4. helio = sun   heliology, helioscope, heliosis
5. meter = measure   meter, pedometer, seismometer
6. chron = time   chronic, chronology, chronicle
7. omni = all   omnibus, omnipotent, omnivorous
8. pre = before   preamble, predict, precedent
9. apo = away from   apogee, apology, apothegm
10. cred = believe   creditable, accreditation, creed
11. ize = to make   familiarize, fertilize, centralize
12. non = not   nontoxic, nonsense, nonpartisan
13. anthrop = man   anthropology, philanthropy
14. neur = nerve   neurology, neurosis, neurotic
15. migra = wander   migration, immigrant, emigrate
16. tele = distance/far   telephone, telecommunications
17. scope = to see   microscope, telescope, periscope
18. photo = light   photograph, photokinesis, photology

FIGURE 10–4   Morphemes Determine Word Meaning

1.	automobile	auto = self
		mobile = moveable
2.	telephone	tele = distant/far
		phone = sound
3.	microscope	micro = small
		scope = to see
4.	biology	bio = life
		ology = the study of
5.	orthodontist	ortho = straight
		dont = teeth
		ist = a person who
6.	autobiography	auto = self
		bio = life
		graph = to write
7.	transport	trans = across
		port = to carry
8.	homograph	homo = same
		graph = to write
9.	chromophobic	chromo = color
		phobic = fear of
10.	geology	geo = earth
		ology = the study of
11.	populicide	pop = people
		cide = to kill
12.	polyglot	poly = many
		glot = tongue
13.	bilingual	bi = two
		lingual = language
14.	pseudonym	pseudo = false
		nym = name

Brainstorming

Brainstorming

Brainstorming literally means to storm the brain. By brainstorming, you are attempting to create a spontaneous flow of thoughts. The purpose is to produce a flood of ideas.

Companies use brainstorming techniques to come up with ideas for new products or advertising strategies. Citizen groups use brainstorming to create solutions to community problems. School systems use brainstorming to generate new ideas for curricula and reorganization. You may have been part of a group that used brainstorming to solve a problem by spontaneously contributing ideas and then making decisions based on your best thoughts.

Brainstorming and Organization

Brainstorming is the first and most important step in getting organized. Brainstorming takes a small amount of thinking time, but can save you a great amount of production time when you set out to do a project or activity. Brainstorming is often overlooked and deemed to be unessential. However, if you are interested in saving valuable time in an already jam-packed schedule, you must not neglect brainstorming.

Group Brainstorming

Group brainstorming often produces a greater variation in ideas due to the synergism that is created when more than one person is involved. So, if you have classmates or friends who are willing to brainstorm with you, it would be beneficial.

"Now do we all have our thinking caps on?"

Reprinted by permission: Bob Brown

Individual Brainstorming

If, however, there is no one but you, brainstorming is still effective. Begin by making, and taking, time to think. Find a place that is conducive to thinking. Then, set aside a block of time so you don't feel rushed. Remember, it takes time for the brain to know what it is you are trying to generate. Consequently, your best solutions or ideas will often come after you think you have thought of every possible idea that could exist. Be patient! Brainstorming is as much a process as a product.

Brainstorming Guidelines

You will need a conducive atmosphere for brainstorming. Most people do their best thinking in an atmosphere free from distractions. So find a quiet, comfortable place where you won't be interrupted. You will need pencil and paper, or you may wish to use a word processor.

As soon as an idea comes to your mind, write it down. Do not evaluate it. Do not judge it to be significant, or insignificant. Otherwise, you will defeat the purpose of brainstorming. Just write continuously and do not stop to edit. There are no right, or wrong, answers and the order is not important. The object of brainstorming is to produce a spontaneous flow of ideas that can be used to help you effectively produce a desired product. You won't be in a position to know what ideas will be valuable until you have them all listed. So, just write them down.

At some later point in time you will be selecting the ideas that you think are valuable and which you chose to use. For example, if you have a term paper to write or a teaching demonstration to perform, you will use the brainstorming technique to help you think of what ideas you might include and how they will fit together. If you eliminate creative thoughts early in the brainstorming process, you may throw away the very thought that could make your project unique.

Practicing the Technique

If you haven't had any experience in brainstorming, spend some time practicing. Think of an object such as a bathtub, a pencil, or a paper clip. List all of the ways that you can think of in which this object could be used. In the beginning, your ideas may be quite common. However, observe how your creativity changes as you list more and more ideas.

The following examples are listed to stimulate your thinking and help you to see how the process works.

Problem: What are some uses for a bathtub?

1. a bathtub
2. a bed
3. a place to read
4. a place to hide
5. a flowerpot
6. a birdbath
7. a punch-bowl

8. a litterbox
9. a storage chest
10. a laundry bin
11. a little kid's pool
12. a patio garden
13. a big fish bowl
14. a wagon
15. an animal cage
16. a sandbox
17. a playhouse
18. a terrarium

Now, it is time for you to practice. Here's a problem for you to brainstorm, or you may prefer to think of one of your own.

Problem: What are some ways to use a paper clip?

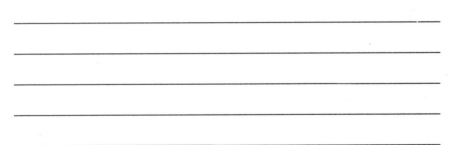

Brainstorming for Subdividing

The basic purpose of brainstorming is to generate ideas through a process of free association. In relationship to organization, the reason for doing this is to help you to recognize possible solutions, identify alternative perspectives, and, in addition, specify the smaller parts of the bigger task.

Often assignments such as term projects or research papers seem like monumental tasks. This is one of the reasons that they are often put off longer than they should be. It doesn't have to be this way. Moreover, simpler tasks that you may find difficult don't have to be neglected because you don't know where to begin. Remember, just the act of writing down your brainstorming ideas is a beginning. You've started; you're on your way!

Brainstorming can help you divide a larger goal into its more manageable parts, so that the task will seem less overwhelming.

First, define the goal and write it at the top of a sheet of paper or on your word processor. Next, begin to make a list of all the things you can think of that will need to be done in order to complete the goal.

Unblocking Blocked Ideas

If you have trouble generating ideas, here are several unblocking techniques, used by writers, to help you release the floodgates so your ideas will flow.

1. Keep Writing
Keep your pencil on the paper, or your hands on the keyboard. Don't stop writing. If you can't think of an idea related to your goal, then write something else. Write your grocery list, write the days of the week, write the alphabet—write anything, but just keep writing. Often, the trouble is not beginning, but continuing! So, keep the brain in the writing mode by continuing to write.

2. Use a Tape Recorder
If you find that you can express your ideas orally more easily than in written form, you may want to tape-record your ideas. Dictate your ideas on a tape recorder, play them back, and transcribe them.

3. Use a Scribe or Ask a Friend to Help
Ask someone to write down your ideas as you speak them. Sometimes your ideas get blocked because you cannot write as fast as you can think. Someone else who writes quickly can get your ideas in print so your energies can be reserved for creative thinking.

4. Write a Letter to a Friend
If you are brainstorming in order to get started on a very important project, the pressure of beginning may cut off some of your creative juices. One of the ways you can take the pressure off of yourself is to pretend that you are writing to a friend. So, rather than putting your ideas in the form of a list, put them in the form of a letter.

Here is an example of this technique.

Dear Angie,

I have to clean my room, but I don't know where to begin. It seems like I have so much junk. Where does it all come from? The task seems overwhelming!

I know I need to throw some stuff away. I have notebooks and old handouts from last term that I no longer need. If I put all my dirty laundry in the clothes bag, I could see the floor of my closet and likely find my tennis shoes. Maybe if I got a laundry basket, I could throw my clothes in, even if I were on the other side of the room. My clothes bag is such a pain. It is too tiny. I also need to get some more hangers, so I don't just toss my clothes on the back of the chair.

Have you heard from Karlene? Bye for now!

Love, Valerie

Perhaps the informality of writing a letter to a friend will allow you to get some of your ideas on paper without feeling the pressure of performing. The format is immaterial since generating ideas is the key purpose of this technique.

5. Ask for Help

Sometimes it helps to have help! Don't be reluctant to ask someone to help you brainstorm. It may be that your ideas aren't flowing because you lack confidence or because you are evaluating your ideas before they are recorded. The ideas, support, and encouragement of a friend or family member are worth the asking.

6. Reevaluate Your Physical and Mental Preparation

Reevaluate your external and internal preparation for brainstorming. Do you have your tools— paper, pencil, tapes, batteries? Are you in an environment free of distractions? Have you determined a block of time for brainstorming? Not being prepared is often an excuse for not doing an activity. Appropriate preparation will make it easier to get the task started. And, once started, it is easier to keep going.

7. Don't Quit

If at first you don't succeed, change your pace or perspective, but don't quit! You may need to take a break or do some relaxation exercises to ease your tension. Just remember that brainstorming is a process. It takes time. Don't give up too easily. However, if you are not having any success after many attempts, it may be best to return to this activity at another time.

12

Notetaking

Key Aspects of Notetaking

It is reasonable to expect that you will spend twelve or more hours per week attending lectures. Needless to say, you will be getting a lot of auditory information. Unless you have a magnificent auditory memory, it will be necessary for you to take notes.

1. Meaning Vocabulary
It is not enough to simply hear the words spoken by the professor during a class lecture. You need to comprehend the meaning of the words and the ideas they convey. Thus, work diligently to learn the specialized vocabulary for each subject so you will understand what is being said.

2. Attention
When you are in class, put all other distractions aside and give your undivided attention to the content of the lecture. Assume that the information you receive in each of your lecture classes is some of the most important information you will ever get. You will be much more successful if you make it a habit of becoming absorbed into the world of each subject you study.

3. Activate Listening
Notetaking is not a substitute for listening! Before you can take good notes, you must listen well. Tune in to what you are hearing. Activating your listening will enhance your learning.

4. Preview the Content
Before you attend class, preview the material to be presented. You might choose to read it thoroughly, particularly if you have limited

prior knowledge of the subject. Or, you may choose to skim the material just before you attend the lecture.

5.   Balance Listening and Writing

Knowing how to recognize the main idea and glean the key points is an extremely important skill when you are reading or listening. There should be a good balance between the time you spend listening and the time you spend writing. Weigh the importance of the information. Listen for cues such as "three major categories are," "the main idea is," or "in summary."

Sometimes it is good to record the words of the professor as they were used. However, it is also important that you record relevant remarks in your own words. The key is that you understand what is being said and that your notes are written in such a manner that you will understand them later.

Be alert to any techniques that your professor uses to present information. For example, some information may be summarized on a transparency or given to you in the form of a handout.

6. Lecture Notes

Take notes in outline form or in a modified form of outlining. If the lecture is not delivered in a manner that is easily outlined, then do not spend valuable time trying to determine the main points and the supporting details. Instead, just make a list of the important ideas and number them consecutively. If it is apparent that some points are subordinate ideas, then indent and list them under the main idea.

Review lecture notes as soon after the class finishes as is possible. Use this opportunity to reflect on the day's lecture and fill in any pieces of information that you remember but neglected to include in your notes.

Coding Symbols for Notetaking

The following symbols are suggested for you to use as a code for one or more words. These coding symbols will help you increase the speed with which you can take notes during lectures or read-

+	plus, and	...	repeats same pattern
-	minus	&	and
*	important	w/	with
def	definition	w/o	without
#	number, pounds	ex	example
@	at, and	ie	that it, therefore
$	dollars, money	re	regarding
%	percent	s	summary
=	equals, is related to	etc.	and so forth; in addition
"	inches, repeated	4	for
'	feet	be/4	before
2	to, too, two	vs	versus
p	page	wd	word
/g	to indicate "ing"	b/c	because
		cont'd	continued

Many of these symbols are used in a universal coding system.

ing periods. Many of these are standard symbols. Others are de-signed especially for the ease and comprehension of particular words or ideas.

You are encouraged to use these codes, or develop your own sys-tem of abbreviations. However, whatever codes you use, be sure that they are meaningful to you and that they flow easily and naturally.

Alternatives to Independent Notetaking

Some students find it difficult to take notes while listening to lec-tures. Thus, much information is lost. When this situation occurs, one should consider alternatives. The following are some sugges-tions to supplement your notes:

Notetakers

1. Ask a fellow student to take notes for you. This can be done by using a carbon or by making xerox copies of the original notes.
2. Ask the professor to arrange for a student in the class to vol-unteer to be the class notetaker. The notes are placed in a central location immediately after class so the notes can be picked up.
3. Ask the appropriate staff person within the university to make arrangements for a notetaker. Sometimes the univer-sity will provide professional student notetakers on a paid, or volunteer, basis.

Taped Lectures

CAUTION: Get permission from the professor before taping a lec-ture. In some situations you may be requested to sign a formal statement indicating that the tapes will be used only for your study purposes.

Often it is helpful to tape lectures so they can be listened to in the privacy of a quiet, non-distracting atmosphere. However, re-member that it takes time to play back lectures on a tape record-ing. Thus, you might consider the following suggestions:

1. Use a different tape for each class.
2. Use 120-minute tapes so you won't have to change tapes.
3. Label the tape with the date, topic, and name of the lecturer.
4. Use rechargeable batteries so you will not be confined to a seating location that has an electrical outlet.
5. Use the pause button. Tape only the essential information.
6. Set the counter on the tape recorder at zero. Make note of the counter number when a key point is given. Then, when you listen to the lecture, you will be alert to noting the main ideas. Also, this procedure will dictate that you keep tuned in and be an active listener.
7. Review the tape as soon as possible after the lecture. Make any necessary additions to your notes.

Memory

Our Memory at Work

Memory is one of our most remarkable capacities. As human beings, we have the ability to think. In addition, we possess mental storage and retrieval systems that, potentially, are far more efficient in their capacity, flexibility, and power than the most up-to-date computers.

Reprinted with special permission of King Features Syndicate.

Processing Information

A major function of memory is to organize and process information. Different parts of the brain process different elements of an experience as we undergo it. This information is then classified for storage so that it can be reassembled later on with all of its complex detail.

Sensory Input

The pace and technology of our modern life exposes us to an overwhelming amount of sensory input on a daily basis. Seeing, hearing, touching, tasting, and smelling connect us to the world in which we live. Each of our senses is a complex collection of receptor cells that send out different sorts of electrical signals to the brain. Thus, our senses are the tools that enable us to discover and explore the world around us.

How to Remember

A good way to remember how memory works is to think of these Rs: Remembering, Registration, Retention, and Retrieval (recall and recognition).

Registration

The brain is constantly bombarded with thousands of pieces of information being collected by our sensory system. The process of registration, or acquisition, consists of recognizing these pieces of relevant stimuli and working to give them meaning so they can be understood and stored into memory.

Registration relates closely to selective attention. You can't remember what you don't recognize or register. Acquisition also is highly dependent upon exposure. The more experiences you have, the greater the knowledge base you will develop. This knowledge base becomes the glue by which new information is attached.

Retention

Rehearsal is an important component of retention. Memorizing information consists of both overt and covert repetition of information to register it more firmly into memory. Two aspects of rehearsal are maintenance and elaboration. In maintenance, you repeat the information over and over. In elaboration, you create rich associations to make the information more meaningful. It is at this stage that mnemonics clearly enhance rehearsal and facilitate subsequent retrieval.

Retrieval

Learning is one thing, but remembering or retrieving what you have learned can be something entirely different. Retention and retrieval strategies complement each other. Thus, the stronger the memory imprint, the greater the probability of accurate recall at a later time.

The Reality

In academic situations you must recognize that grades are a reflection of what can be shown, not necessarily what is actually known. It may seem unfair, but if you can't recall or recognize facts or concepts while taking tests, the practical results are the same as if you had never studied in the first place. Knowing that you know the information is not enough. You must be able to retrieve what you know!

Stages or Types of Memory

Memory is not a single system. Instead, it consists of several interconnected systems that work together. There are basically three types of memory systems or stages through which information can progress.

   1. *Sensory Memory.* Sensory memory is very brief—about three seconds. Its purpose is exemplified by the ability to hold the beginning letters of a word in memory while reading the ending letters, so you can pronounce the entire word.
   2. *Short-Term Memory.* Short-term memory, although a little longer, holds information in a temporary storage, just long enough to carry out a particular task, such as dialing an unfamiliar telephone number. The duration of short-term memory is about thirty seconds. Its basic purpose is to give you time to decide whether to

use it or lose it. If you don't want to remember a particular piece of information, do nothing. If, however, you want to use it, you must rehearse it in some manner to move it into the next phase, which is long-term memory.

3. *Long-Term Memory.* Long-term memory is used to remember information for long periods of time. As far as we know, its capacity is unlimited and its duration is forever.

Write It Down

It is a myth to think that you can remember everything that you want to remember. How many times have you said, "Oh, I'll remember that!" only to forget it when you wanted to recall it. We all have been guilty of this mistake. The problem is that we repeat the mistake over and over again!

How do we break this habit? Perhaps it is best to begin by changing the perception that only old people forget. Since you probably don't consider yourself old, you may have the idea that, of course, you will remember. And, more often than not, you will. But, what if you don't? Why take the chance? Write it down!

Lee Iacocca wrote in his autobiography, "The discipline of writing something down is the first step to making it happen." Think about it. If you write it down, you are more likely to get it done. Successful people everywhere make lists, write notes, or keep journals. These are all acts of writing it down.

It would be terrific if there were a lost and found area in the brain like those we have in schools and other locations. If you lost an idea, you could go to the lost and found and retrieve it. However, some ideas are like fragile bubbles; if you don't do something to preserve them, they may pop and be gone forever.

As you practice the art of writing it down, you may discover a wonderful dividend—you will experience more ideas with less effort and worry. There are a number of reasons why this happens. First, you aren't using valuable brain energy trying to hang on to that memory. You know that you have that thought recorded and you are, therefore, free to think of other things! Second, when you write it down, you let it simmer for a period of time. Some thoughts need time to incubate. As you review your notes at another point in time, you may find that you see the task or problem differently or have new ideas to add to the original thought.

So, keep a pocket notebook handy at all times. Put one in your car, in your backpack, in your purse, on your desk, and beside your bed. You never know when you will hear or think of something that you will want to remember. Dispel the I won't forget attitude.

The physical act of writing assists memory in that it is a kinesthetic/tactile activity. In these days of intense academic study you will have lots to remember, so be wise and write it down. Develop the notion that writing it down will assist your memory, help you generate more ideas, and save you time!

Chunking

George Miller of Harvard University, in an influential paper, "The Magical Number Seven: Plus or Minus Two," pointed out that the immediate memory span was limited in the number of items it could hold (Miller 1956, p. 81–97).

He found that whether people were given lists of numbers or words, they had difficulty recalling more than about seven items. This is not surprising because it fits in with the fact that you are unlikely to be able to sub-vocalize more than seven items in less than ten seconds. It should be noted that seven is also the approximate capacity of short-term memory storage.

Miller's contribution was to point out that the number of items was the limiting factor—not the information contained in those items. Thus, by increasing the amount of information in each item, you can remember more. In other words, while much information can be packed into chunks, don't try to remember too many chunks.

Chunking is a natural process. Consider the number 3294027. If you chunk it into two parts, you have a typical telephone number: 329 4027. Two chunks are much easier to remember than seven individual numbers. Or, consider memorizing this social security number: 341448970. It is easier to remember if you break it into these chunks: 341 44 89 70; or these chunks: 341 44 8970.

Magic seven seems to be a universal phenomenon! It is a valuable tool to use when you are memorizing lists or groups of

Reprinted by permission: Tribune Media Services.

things. Remember, this concept is not limited to remembering numbers; it can also be used with words. For example, if you have to memorize a list of twenty vocabulary words, group or organize them into chunks that are meaningful to you or, have a pattern. Just remember to make each group or chunk no longer than about seven items.

Peg System Using Numerical Associations

The *Peg System* is a way to help you memorize and retain information from a list that must be learned in a specific sequence. For illustrative purposes, let's limit our example to ten pegs, sometimes called key words. These ten words will be attached to a number, which acts like a peg. You will need to think about the associations until they become meaningful and then rehearse them so they will be locked into permanent memory. When you have them in permanent memory, you will be able to use them for any list of ten items that you need to remember.

Here are ten pegs that have been found meaningful (Olney 1988, p. 20).

1. won
2. two
3. tree
4. star
5. foot
6. six-pack
7. Seven-Up

8. ate
9. nine-iron
10. tent

These are the associations that I use for the key words to make the pegs meaningful. (1) Won is a homonym that provides some action. (2) Two gives a number. (3) Tree is three with the h left out. (4) Star is associated with a four-star general or a four-star hotel or restaurant. (5) Foot is connected to the song "Five foot two, eyes of blue..." (6) Six-pack is related to a six-pack beverage. (7) Seven-Up reminds me of a favorite soda. (8) Ate is the homonym for the number eight. (9) A nine-iron is associated with golf. (10) Finally, tent is ten with a t added to form an item that can be easily visualized.

As with any general system for memorizing, it has value only when it is applied. For example, let's assume you needed to know the presidents of the United States in chronological order. Just in case you have forgotten, the first ten presidents are: Washington, Adams, Jefferson, Madison, Monroe, Adams, Jackson, Van Buren, Harrison, and Tyler.

Now that you know the pegs and can recall them immediately, you need to spend a little time forming your associations with the names of the presidents.

Remember that there are many ways to form meaningful associations, such as using alliteration, visualization, action, and ridiculous humor. Here is one example:

1. Washington won the war. This association uses won and it also incorporates alliteration.
2. There were two Adams.
3. Jefferson is climbing a tree. Or Jefferson's son is in the tree. Remember, associations don't have to be real or logical.
4. Madison is connected to the stars of Madison Avenue. Madison Square Garden and boxing are associated since you may see stars when you get knocked out.
5. Monroe is rowing his boat with his feet on Monday. Keep in mind that the brain seems to enjoy the ridiculous when it comes to memory.
6. Adams appears twice so they got a six-pack to celebrate.

7. Jackson's son Jack likes Seven-Up.
8. Van Buren ate eight burritos in his van.
9. Harry was playing golf with his son who was using a nine-iron.
10. Tyler was sleeping in a tent.

Once you have formed your individual associations, you may choose to link several sentences together to form a longer story. Be sure to visualize the action of the story and add a little emotion to personalize it and, thus, lock it into meaningful memory. Drawing pictures of each association may also be helpful.

For You to Do: Make a list of your own pegs to use with the Peg System.

1.

2.

3.

4.

5.

6.

7.

8.

9.

10.

Peg System Using Rhyme

The peg system is a technique that can be used to help you memorize and retain information that must be learned in a specific sequence. Some peg sets emphasize numerical relationships. This peg system uses the rhyme of the language to create the key association for each peg or memory hook. It might be a good idea to memorize both sets so that you will have some options when you are confronted with memory work that involves a series of items that need to be associated.

These are the following pegs that you would put into permanent memory.

1. bun
2. shoe
3. tree
4. door
5. hive
6. stick
7. heaven
8. gate
9. line
10. hen

These peg words are best learned in a phrase such as:

1. One is a bun.
2. Two is a shoe.
3. Three is a tree.
4. Four is a door.
5. Five is a hive.
6. Six is a stick.
7. Seven is heaven.
8. Eight is a gate.
9. Nine is a line.
10. Ten is a hen.

Points to Remember:

1. A peg system is best memorized by imaging the association in a realistic or humorous manner.
2. It is best to use single nouns.
3. Concrete nouns are preferable to abstract ones.

4. It is best to use nouns that are meaningful to you or that follow a pattern that is easily remembered.
5. You may use the linking system to connect several pegs together in a chunk or group.

Checklist of Memory Techniques

The following is a list of key ideas and techniques that can be used to remind you of some of the many strategies for enhancing memory.

1. Association: Connect a new idea to a previous idea.
2. Prior knowledge: The more you know about a subject the better your memory will function as you learn new information.
3. Chunking: Categorize quantities of information in groups.
4. Numbered lists: The brain likes numbers.
5. Acronyms: Words can be sensical or non-sensical.
6. Acrostics: Creative sentences.
7. Picture Memory: Drawing concrete pictures and using visualization or imagery.
8. Color coding: To categorize and discriminate.
9. Personalize information.
10. Pretend you're the expert.
11. Dramatize information.
12. Muscle/Movement Memory: Use upper body movement to access kinesthetic memory.
13. Finger Memory: Touch a finger for each piece of information.
14. Organize the information in a logical/memorable manner.
15. Use ridiculous humor: The brain likes to laugh.
16. Use frequent exposures to information over a long period of time.
17. Flash cards: Carry them with you.
18. Repetition: Make it meaningful.
19. SQ3R Study Method.
20. Time on task: The more you study, the more you learn.
21. Peg System: Memorize a series of pegs and attach new information to those pegs.
22. Loci System: Use a series of familiar locations and associate new information with the locations.

23. Locational Memory: Vary the places where you study.
24. Rhyme.
25. Music.
26. Framing key words: Highlight, Circle, or Square helps eyes to stay within the frame and focus on the word.
27. Semantic Mapping.
28. Linking: Connecting one idea to another so one triggers the other.
29. Story Memory: Tell a story using all the salient points that you wish to remember.
30. Patterns: Look for a logical pattern, a generalization, or a rule for that which is to be memorized.
31. Alliteration.
32. Categorization: Assists in focus and location of information.
33. Paired-association: Connecting in pairs like Lansing-Michigan or auto-self.
34. Visualization/Imagery: Create a motion picture of the chunks of information to be learned.
35. Self-testing: Give yourself feedback by making up tests, or practice writing essays.
36. Ask Questions! Search for the answers!

Remember these important keys:
 See it! Say it! Do it!
 Read it! Write it! Repeat it!
 Oliver Wendell Holmes: "A man must get a thing before he can forget it."

14

Tests

Test Anxiety

Some test anxiety may not be negative for it may urge you to organize your time and responsibilities so you will study more. However, too much anxiety can be detrimental to effective performance on examinations.

Use the following as a checklist to determine if your anxiety is becoming excessive.

1. Insomnia/Not sleeping well.
2. Feeling nervous.
3. Blocking information.
4. Headaches.
5. Waking up early.
6. Stomach and/or intestinal problems.
7. Depression.
8. Panic attacks.
9. Thinking you don't know.
10. Worried you won't be able to think logically.
11. Afraid there won't be enough time to review.
12. Feeling out of control.
13. Uncertainty/Not being able to make decisions.
14. Not eating, or eating too much.
15. Hyperactivity.

16. Feelings of despair.
17. Excessive forgetting.
18. Mood swings.
19. Crying easily/Anger.
20. _____
Add personalized statements that are not reflected on the list.

If you find you are, or are becoming, too anxious, decide to seek informal help or professional counseling.

Counteracting Test Anxiety

In many ways, test anxiety is a natural part of being a college student. However, when anxiety becomes excessive, it can lead to a dysfunction or decreased academic performance.

It is up to you to take charge and do things that will decrease your anxiety and bring it into proper perspective. The following are some suggestions to help you with your thinking. (Remember to consult a physician or other appropriate professional for concerns that may be beyond the normal stress of taking exams.)

Difficulty with Sleep

1. Keep a regular schedule as often as possible. If you find it necessary to change your schedule, try to change it at least a week before exams, so you will be slightly adjusted to it before the actual week of examinations.

For example, if you know that you are going to have several 8 A.M. exams and you are not used to getting up that early, begin the week before exams to get up at 6:30 A.M., or 7:00 A.M., so your body will have time to adjust to the change.

2. Eat the right food. Give your body the proper nutrition so it can work for you and not against you. Under stress, you may be more prone to illnesses that will hinder your academic performance.

3. Eliminate caffeine and other such elements that may interfere with your sleep.

4. Exercise to reduce stress. Physical activity uses a different type of energy than does studying. Physical exercise uses energy that makes you physically fatigued and, therefore, assists you in falling asleep.

Headaches

1. Place a cold compress on your forehead or over your eyes. Relax.

2. Cup your hands over your eyes. Open your eyes into the darkness of your hands. This will ease the strain.

3. Gently massage the head, neck, and shoulder area. Your tenseness may be causing a decrease in circulation.

4. Avoid the kinds of foods that may cause your headaches.

Depression

1. Consult a professional who is qualified to assist you with this difficulty.

Waking Up Early

1. Stay in bed and rest. Consider listening to pleasant music.

2. Get up and make good use of your time.

Not Eating or Eating Too Much

1. Eat properly.

2. Avoid junk food.

3. Acknowledge a change in your eating behaviors.
Recognition of the change is often sufficient to bring it back into control. If the eating behavior change is not radical, it may not be significant. Just remember that the body functions on nutrients, so don't neglect your body. You can't do your best performance if you are not feeling well.

Hyperactivity

1. Use relaxation exercises and tapes.

2. Exercise physically.

Knowledge and Thinking Concerns

1. Study effectively over a long period of time. This is the best remedy for concerns about knowing the information. If you have studied hard and well, you will most likely know the information.

2. Keep relaxed. Being in a relaxed state will help you effectively use your thinking and reasoning powers.
3. Have confidence in your abilities. Believe in yourself.
4. Use self-talk. Repeat positive affirmations.

Mood Swings/Emotional Concerns

1. Recognize that this is a time of stress and that it is natural to have some shifts in your emotional state.
2. Avoid people and events that may elevate negative feelings or add to your stress. Keep your stress level as minimal as possible.

Time

1. Determine that there is enough time to do what you need to do.
2. Plan in advance so you won't be overloaded in the days preceding your examinations.
3. Use your time wisely. Study smart!

Blocking and Forgetting

1. Relaxation releases energy for learning and thinking.
2. Trust your memory. Practice retrieving information the same way you rehearsed storing it.
3. Practice examinations on your own; make up exam questions and answer them. Write out information in essay style. This type of exercise will reveal what you know and what you don't know. Learn what you don't know.
4. Use visualization. Pretend that you are taking the examination. Role play the examination situation in your mind. This will be like a dress rehearsal. Having experienced the examination in your mind, you may not be as anxious when you are actually taking the exam in that you already feel familiar with the task.

   Be sure to give yourself a good grade when you take the test in your mind. You might want to say, "Yea! Yea! I

Reprinted by permission: Tribune Media Services.

earned an A." Make a physical record of the grade you
would like to earn.

Attention

The above suggestions are given to stimulate your thinking about
ways you can keep test anxiety within an appropriate context. It is
always important to know yourself and know your body. Be wise
and logical in the behaviors that you practice. Think positive
thoughts and affirm your chances for success. Seek professional
counsel when appropriate.

Conquering the Fear of Taking Tests

For many students, taking a test is just another part of the academic protocol. However, for some students, the worry, anxiety, or
fear that taking a test elicits is overwhelming!

A test-anxious student may do poorly on an exam even though
he or she knows the material. Blocking or blanking out during an
exam is a common response, despite the fact that the student has
spent hours studying.

What Causes Test Anxiety?

Test anxiety may be caused by pressure, past experiences, the fear
of failure, or the fear of success. Consider the following statements:

1. "I am so stupid; I'll never pass this test."
2. "If I don't pass this test, I'll flunk the course."
3. "I never do well no matter how much I study."

4. "My parents are paying for my education. I can't let them down."
5. "My brothers and sisters are smarter than I am. They get better grades."
6. "What will my teacher think?"

You Can Learn to Control Your Emotions

1. Think about why you become anxious and afraid.
2. Recognize that negative thoughts inhibit production.
3. Counteract irrational thoughts with rational counter-thoughts.
4. Remember that your imagination is capable of thinking about positive as well as negative happenings.
5. Learn to relax.

Preparation for the Test

1. Studying for long-term retention is the best preparation for taking a test. It is important to space your studying so you will have time to process information and utilize memory techniques effectively.
2. Find out what kind of test you will be taking and study accordingly. Predict the questions that might be on the exam. Look at previous tests given by the instructor and review the self-tests that may be in the textbook.
3. Make every effort to be at your best when taking the test. Adequate rest, nourishment, and physical comforts are an important part of preparation for test taking.
4. Confidence is crucial. Confidence comes with knowing that you are prepared.

General Test-Taking Tips

1. Get a good night's sleep the night before the exam.
2. Have something to eat the morning of the exam.
3. Dress nicely for the exam. Wear your favorite colors.
4. Arrive at the exam early and get a good seat.

5. Don't crash study just before the test. This may cause confusion. Allow your brain time to relax.
6. Look over the whole test so you can budget your time according to the value of the questions.
7. Use all the time allotted to take the exam. Even if you just sit for a while, some information may be accessed during this time.

Objective Examinations

1. Study more to memorize information and concentrate on details.
2. Look for signal or cue words such as always, never, often, basically, sometimes, and all.
3. Take care not to add words and ideas that are not stated.
4. Remember not to ignore critical qualifiers such as may, should, must, and so forth.
5. Elimination of incorrect or definitely inadequate answers can narrow the field of choice.
6. Don't waste time third guessing what the test designer might have meant. Read and relate to the words that are there.
7. When matching items, match the ones you know first, then match the ones you are unsure of or do not know.
8. Read items with double and triple negatives very carefully. Pause after each section and think about what that portion means; then, synthesize the whole statement.
9. Don't assume a piece of information is a typing error unless it is obvious. Most typing errors will be in the spelling of words.
10. When you recognize a statement taken directly from the book, read carefully to be sure that the instructor has not shifted the wording.
11. Statements with specific determiners such as none or all are rarely true.
12. Statements with specific determiners such as most or generally are frequently true.

13. True-false items may be determined by one word, a specific number, or a specific noun.
14. Some multiple-choice questions are searching for the best choice rather than the right choice. Several choices may be right, but there will be one that is most right.

Multiple-Choice Examinations

1. Use two blank sheets of paper: cover the questions above and below the one you are answering. This will help you to focus.
2. Look over the whole exam quickly before beginning to answer specific questions. Determine how long the test is so that you can apportion your time appropriately.
3. Answer the easiest questions first. If you get frustrated with one section, go to a different section that may be easier for you. This will encourage you and may help you get your brain functioning if that is the problem.
4. Don't dwell on difficult questions. Make a decision about an answer and return to it later to reconsider your choice.
5. Use the process of elimination. Each time you eliminate an answer that is not correct, you increase your chances of getting the right answer.
6. Read the question and determine the answer before you search the multiple choice options. Then, search for your answer. If your answer is not there, you must choose from those that are close to your answer.
7. Search for key words that give meaning to the question or the answer. Focus on nouns, verbs, and objects, including indirect objects, direct objects, and objects of prepositions.
8. Be aware of words that specify, such as always, never, often, not, and so forth.
9. Use context, reasoning, and logic to figure out the questions you don't readily know.
10. Recognize that some questions may provide the answers, or clues to the answers, to other questions.
11. Use your intuition to help you select an answer if you have no idea which is a feasible response.

"I looked at the first essay question and my whole life passed before my eyes."

Reprinted by permission: Mike Streff

12. Collect data. If on previous tests you changed answers that were usually correct, then consider not changing an answer unless you are sure.

13. Consider answering multiple-choice questions by thinking of each choice as being true or false in relationship to the question.

14. Pause throughout the test to take some deep breaths and stretch you neck and shoulder muscles.

Essay Examinations

1. Use multiple-choice statements to give you ideas for answers to essay questions.
2. Be sure you know what the essay question is asking. Focus your attention on key verbs such as compare, contrast, describe, and list.
3. Jot down any ideas that come to mind and then think about how you might organize those thoughts.
4. Always explain your main ideas with supporting details. Include a clincher statement.
5. Write as much as you know.

Study Smart!   Believe In Yourself!!   You Can Do It!!!

15

Professors

Relationships with Professors

As a student, you will have a special relationship with your professors. This does not necessarily mean that it will be personal or wonderful. Rather, it means that it will be one that requires good working dynamics of the same nature as those in best friend interactions.

Professors are people, too, and if you learn the skills that are conducive to good friendships, you will have a distinct advantage when you interact with your professors.

Here are some important principles to put at the top of your list.

1. Attend Class Regularly

If you are registered for a class, the professor expects you to attend. Be there!

Some students make the mistake of thinking that they do not have to attend class if they don't want to. Their reasoning is that, since they are paying tuition to take the class, they can determine whether or not they attend. This is immature thinking.

Attend class regularly and, if possible, arrive early. Use this time to interact with the professor or your fellow classmates. If you don't care to interact, review your notes or just relax. Your attendance and lack of tardiness will help to demonstrate a commitment to excellence.

If you are still not convinced that you should attend class regularly, check the policy on attendance recorded in your university bulletin. Often, unknown to students, the professor..."is authorized to lower scholastic ratings if the student's absences or latenesses require this action...." (CMU Bulletin 1993–1994, p. 95).

2. Be Attentive

Most professors practice good eye contact with their students, so it is important that you are attentive in class. Sleeping, daydreaming, or activities such as writing letters are inappropriate behaviors for the serious student.

Even more inappropriate is conversing with your neighbor while the professor is speaking. This is viewed as a personal insult to the instructor and it also disturbs the other students. Besides, you will miss what is being said and it may be vital information. The temptation to talk is often great, but make it a practice to avoid temptation.

3. Participate in Class Discussions and Activities

Like good friendships, teaching and learning is a two-way street. Teachers are expected to teach and learners are expected to learn. You will have a better chance of learning if you participate actively in class discussions and activities.

You may have become conditioned, over the years, to interact very infrequently during class discussions. This lack of interaction will not do! You must change!

Often, students do not ask questions or volunteer to answer those that are asked. This gives the impression that you do not know or you aren't willing to participate—both leave negative impressions.

Participating in class gives the impression that you are prepared and interested in advancing your own knowledge. Just as you remember those with whom you converse more often, professors, too, remember those who participate, due to the more frequent one-to-one interaction. Thus, they are more likely to make a greater investment in developing that special student-teacher bonding. Asking questions or making comments just to be noticed, however, wastes class time and often has a negative impact.

4. Cultivate a Positive Attitude Toward Class

Your attitude can make or break your performance in a class. Students talk about professors and you may hear conflicting opinions. But, remember, that is just what it is—an opinion. A bad teacher for another may be the best teacher for you. We all learn differently and have personality preferences. Decide for yourself.

Evaluate your attitude toward the class and/or professor. Be sure that you know full well that your performance can be affected by your attitude. Whether the class/professor is good or bad may be irrelevant. What you learn and what you contribute in class may be more of a reflection of your attitude than the behavior of someone or something else. Besides, a professor may not change to meet your liking, so, ultimately, it will be up to you to take charge.

5. Make an Effort to Help the Professor Know You by Name

Due to the very nature of college, many classes are large and impersonal. A number of your classes will be lecture-style and held in large classrooms or lecture halls.

There will not be much opportunity for the professor to know who you are unless you take the initiative. Do it! Take opportuni-

Reprinted by permission: Glen Dines

ties or make opportunities to interact with your professor in a formal or informal manner. The interaction doesn't have to be long or complex, so don't be intimidated by your lack of confidence in knowing what to do or say. Keep it simple, but genuine.

Early in the semester or term, make an appointment to interact personally and privately with your professor. Many professors have designated office hours for the purpose of interacting with students. Most are delighted to talk to students since that is an integral part of their chosen profession. However, since professors are busy people, make your visit brief. Indicate that your purpose is to introduce yourself. Share some personal goals and/or concerns you have in relationship to the class. Be sincere. You won't be sorry.

6. Learn the Likes and Dislikes of the Professor

Professors are human and have likes and dislikes just as you do. Most of you will acknowledge that dislikes offer greater opportunities for irritations and negative memories. On the contrary, likes open the door for harmony and positive interaction. So, it seems wise to listen to the professor's comments about likes and dislikes and attempt to be in harmony with his or her positive preferences. You may want to read, or reread, the classic book by Dale Carnegie, *How to Win Friends and Influence People.*

7. Arrange for Conferences Before It's Too Late

A conference with your professor may be necessary. Difficulties or differences may arise. Also, additional clarification or input may be needed. Don't wait until the end is near or you're in deep trouble before you seek additional assistance. Seek help early.

Make an appointment. Don't try to solve a problem in the hurried moments before or after class. It may be inappropriate or uncomfortable to deal with a problem in the presence of other students.

If you are meeting with your professor to discuss some differences, don't begin with a personal attack on the professor. Judgments of this nature limit the potential for open and effective communication. Remember it is the teacher's job to judge and evaluate.

Express your complaint in terms of the specific problem rather than a personal attack. For example, "This paper is outstanding and you gave me a C," could be better presented by saying, "I worked hard on this paper and was disappointed that I didn't get a B." Watch your use of I and You messages since You messages often place blame.

Listen to your professor's comments and be willing to discuss your questions and concerns. Ask for what you want. Don't expect your professor to know your wishes. Work for resolution and be willing to negotiate your differences. Be willing to redo your assignment or suggest other solutions that you think would be appropriate.

If you are not satisfied with the resolution of the meeting, you have several options. One is to let it go. Another is to talk to the person at the next level of power. That will often be the department chairperson. If you still are dissatisfied and feel you have a just concern, go to the next higher level. If your concern involves a grade, there is usually a policy and procedure which governs grading grievances.

8. Learn from Your Professors

Professors are an integral part of your education. They have much to teach you. Learn from them. Unless you know it all, there is always something more for you to learn. Respect their knowledge, even if you don't like them or their system of delivery. Learning from the negative can be just as valuable as learning from the positive.

Be a good consumer of the educational opportunities that college offers. Professors will come and go in your life, but your education will be with you forever!

When Professors Talk Fast

Rates of speaking vary. Some people speak fast and others speak slowly. Whatever the rate, one hopes that your listening pace is about the same as the professor's speaking pace. Of course, if you are taking notes, this means that you will need to listen and write as fast as the professor is speaking. If you can do this, then there is no problem. If, however, you can't keep up, here are some suggestions.

1.   Ask permission to record the lecture. However, tape only the information that you want to listen to for a second time. Remember, if you tape for an hour, then you must reserve an hour to listen to the tape. Use the pause button or the stop tab to eliminate the speaking that you don't need to record.

2.   Be willing to ask the professor to repeat information. Also, you might ask the professor to use graphics and/or visual aids to assist you in getting the information that you may miss from the auditory presentation.

3.   Exchange photocopies of class notes with your classmates. It may be wise to copy a set of notes from two different classmates. They will most likely perceive the auditory information differently and have unique ways of recording it.

4.   Be familiar with the subject matter of the lecture. Make an effort to get acquainted with the content to be discussed so you will be in a better position to pick out the key points. The more you know about a subject, the less you will have to focus on each and every word that is spoken.

5.   Focus on key points. Don't try to write everything down. If you get behind, leave a big space. Try to stay with the lecture. Otherwise, you may mix up the information you've already heard because you are writing about something quite different from what you are now hearing.

6.   Leave large empty spaces in your notes if you think you are missing chunks of information because the professor is presenting the information faster than you can record it. Use some type of symbol at this point in your notes so you will be alerted to the fact that you missed some information.

7.   Use more abbreviations than you might normally use. Set aside a time right after class to write out the complete word and fill in any missing points that you remember being discussed.

8.   Be sure to sit in a position within the classroom that will be conducive to good hearing. You may be missing information because the professor is speaking fast, but the problem will be compounded if you can't hear well.

9. If you missed some information, you have several choices. One of them is to ask one of your peers to assist you. Another is to take your notes to the professor and ask for help with the missing chunks of information.

10. Be willing to discuss your needs with the professor. Professors are more than willing to help when asked.

11. Don't panic! You are smart enough to figure out a way to get the information that you need. Be resourceful. You can do it.

16

Learning Disabilities

Be Your Own Best Advocate

In high school, there was probably a greater and more structured support system than you will find in college. Therefore, you must begin immediately to develop your skills for being your own best advocate. You are responsible for your education and, when it comes to the final analysis, you will get what you negotiate.

Be up front about your disability. We all have disabilities in one form or another, so don't think that you are the only one in college with some type of difficulty.

Your professors will expect you to take the initiative in seeking assistance and specialized accommodations. Thus, you will need to make every attempt to understand your specific learning difficulties and discuss them with your professors.

How to Be Your Own Best Advocate

1. Make an Appointment Early
Make an appointment with your professors the first week or two of classes. Don't put it off! Certainly, don't wait until you run into difficulty. This type of timing may appear as if you are trying to weasel out of something.

Also, by consulting with your professors at the very beginning of class, you will be demonstrating your willingness to take the initiative and to be responsible for your own success.

2. Document Your Learning Difficulties

If you have documentation of your learning difficulty, you may want to show the professor a copy of your diagnostic report.

It would be wise to make a list of your learning strengths and weaknesses. Be as specific as possible. Some professors have had little or no experience with college students who have learning disabilities. Thus, you may need to educate them about your specific dysfunction.

3. Anticipate Necessary Accommodations

If you know your specific needs, make a list of accommodations that you anticipate will be necessary and discuss them with your professors. (See the suggested forms, Academic Accommodations for Specialized Learning Needs and the Learning Accommodations Interaction Form, at the end of this section.) Be reasonable and don't ask for any accommodations that are not necessary. If you are not aware of accommodations that could help you function effectively in class, it would be wise to seek counsel.

© 1989, 1990, 1991, 1992 Joel Pett, Lexington Herald-Leader. Reprinted by permission.

4. Remind Your Professor

If you have requested a specific accommodation that is not routine, be sure to remind the professor of your request, particularly if it might require some special arrangements.

5. Use the Resources of the University

There are many resources available in the university community. If you need assistance, be sure to ask. (Record important information on the University Resources form found at the end of this section.)

College Accommodations for the Student With Dyslexia/Learning Disabilities

Students with learning disabilities, either diagnosed or undiagnosed, are entering colleges at an ever-increasing rate. Many will identify themselves. Others will be concerned that they will be unfairly judged if they identify the fact that they have a learning disability. Still others will enter college without the specific knowledge of a learning disability and will not be diagnosed until after they begin their college studies.

Regardless of the circumstances, it is imperative that colleges address the needs of the dyslexic student within the college community. The Office of Civil Rights of the Department of Education requires that every college receiving federal funds of any kind have a Section 504 Coordinator. Section 504 of the Rehabilitation Act of 1973 states that "No otherwise qualified handicapped individual...shall, solely by reason of his handicap, be excluded from the participation in, be denied the benefits of, or be subjected to discrimination under any program or activity receiving federal financial assistance" (Scheiber and Talpers, 1987, viii). Thus, colleges and universities are required to make "reasonable adjustments" to assure that dyslexic students are not excluded from programs because of the absence of ancillary aids.

No two dyslexic students are alike and, thus, not all will need the same accommodations. However, there seem to be some common accommodations that, if provided, are of great value to the dyslexic student and will be invaluable in contributing to the successful completion of a college education. (See Fig. 16–1, 16–2, and 16–3 at the end of this chapter.)

The following is a list of common accommodations that have proved to be invaluable to the dyslexic student. Some are more significant than others because they have a direct impact on the requirements of the college curriculum or the criteria necessary to complete a college degree. Non-dyslexic students may profit little from these accommodations. However, for the dyslexic learner, they may mean the difference between success and failure or acceptable and unacceptable work.

1. *Extended Time on Examinations.* By far the most commonly requested accommodation is extended time on examinations. This is essential due to the slower reading rate and information-processing difficulties of many dyslexic students. Moreover, if the examination should involve writing, more time will be required to conceptualize and organize the written content.

2. *Quiet Location.* Some dyslexic students have also been diagnosed with an Attention Deficit Disorder. This means they will likely have difficulty concentrating because they are easily distracted by background sounds and/or the motion of those around them. Taking examinations in a quiet location, free from distractions, will be imperative if the student is to have a reasonable chance of doing his or her best.

3. *Alternate Forms of Examination.* Multiple-choice examinations may be particularly difficult for some dyslexic students while, for others, writing essay answers presents a real quandary. Some adjustments that may be valuable include: allowing the student to ask for clarification of the written test questions; having the test tape-recorded so it can be processed auditorily as well as visually; furnishing a reader for the examination; and/or allowing the student to be tested by an alternative form of testing.

4. *Use of a Word Processor or Silent Typewriter.* The physical act of writing is difficult for many dyslexic students. Consequently, their writing is often hard to decipher. Also, some students find it easier to record thoughts more quickly if their words can be reproduced mechanically rather than handwritten. Thus, if the physical act of writing presents a significant problem, it would be valuable to allow the student to use a word processor or silent typewriter.

5. *Use of an Electronic Spelling Aid or Dictionary.* It is well documented that correct spelling is a real challenge for dyslexic learners. Thus, if spelling is used as a criterion, it will be a disadvantage if the dyslexic student is restrained from using an appropriate tool to aid in correct spelling.

6. *Examination Accommodations.* Since examinations are a primary means of evaluating success in a college course, it is significant that the student and professor discuss examination accommodations so that the examination results will be a more accurate reflection of the knowledge and achievement of the student.

FIGURE 16–1   Academic Accommodations for Specialized Learning Needs

Student Name:
Student Number:
Address:
Telephone:
Curriculum:
        Major:
        Minor:
Academic Adjustments:
        Class:
        Time:
        Professor:

In an effort to more accurately assess my performance in this class, I am requesting these specific accommodations:

1.   Extended time on examinations
2.   Permission to write on examinations
3.   Use of large print examinations
4.   Use of a dictionary or electronic spelling aid if spelling is evaluated
5.   Use of a quiet area or headphones to block out extraneous noises
6.   Use of an area with limited visual distractions
7.   Use of a reader
8.   Use of a tape recorder
9.   Clarification of directions/assignments
10.   Extended time on project/paper/assignment

Other:

If you would like a reference, please feel free to contact:
        Name:
        Address:
        Telephone:
        Signature:

FIGURE 16–2   Learning Accommodations Interaction Form

TO: (PROFESSOR)   _____

FROM: (STUDENT)   _____

Dear Professor:

     I am enrolled in your class _____
which meets on _____ at _____.

In academic settings, I experience the following difficulties:

  1.

  2.

  3.

  4.

  5.

My learning strengths are:

  1.

  2.

  3.

  4.

  5.

Continued

FIGURE 16–2   (Continued)

To enhance my chances for success in this class, I would benefit from the following accommodations:

1.

2.

3.

If you need further information, please contact me at:

_____

Sincerely,

_____

Date:

_____

FIGURE 16–3   University Resources

The following information should be recorded for quick reference.

1. Academic/Special Services Center:

   Contact Person: _____

   Building: _____   Telephone: _____

2. Counseling Center:

   Counselor: _____

   Building: _____   Telephone: _____

3. Academic Advisor:

   Professor: _____

   Building: _____   Telephone: _____

4. Major Advisor:

   Professor: _____

   Building: _____   Telephone: _____

5. Minor Advisor: _____   _____

   Professor: _____

   Building: _____   Telephone: _____

FIGURE 16–3   (Continued)

6. Office of Student Life:

    Director: _____

    Building: _____   Telephone: _____

7. Department Office:

    Chairperson: _____

    Building: _____   Telephone: _____

Suggestions for College Faculty Interested in Assisting Students with Learning Disabilities

1. Provide students with a detailed course syllabus.
2. Delineate your expectations at the beginning of the course.
3. Start each lecture with an outline of material to be covered. If this isn't possible, visually list the major objectives that will be the focus of the lecture.
4. Briefly summarize the key points at the conclusion of the class.
5. Give directions in specific steps. Be sequential and pause briefly at the beginning of each step. Numbering the steps is beneficial.
6. Present information in visual as well as auditory form.
7. Recognize that students who have specific language disabilities may not be able to take notes as quickly as other students. Allow the student to use a notetaker.
8. Allow students to tape-record the lecture if so desired.
9. Let students choose the best seating location.
10. Permit the students to use aids for spelling.
11. Announce your willingness to assist students who have learning disabilities. Have them identify themselves via written message or make an appointment to discuss their specialized learning needs.
12. Permit students to write on the examination booklet. Identifying the key words in a question or visually crossing out some words is helpful.
13. Make provisions for examinations to be in larger print. Too many words on the page may be disruptive to concentration and comprehension.
14. Allow students extra time on major projects and examinations.
15. Provide a study guide for examinations.
16. View students with learning disabilities as competent and capable students.

17

Suggestions for Success

The following suggestions are gleaned from experiences of students and teachers throughout the nation. Some are personal reflections while others are statements to be considered. Each was considered good advice for any person pursuing academic endeavors.

1. Keep your sense of humor.
2. Get plenty of sleep.
3. Study for long-term memory.
4. Use a pocket organizer.
5. Get a tutor before it's too late.
6. Review your notes right after class.
7. Use flash cards to help you memorize information.
8. Write everything down.
9. Find a quiet place to study.
10. Take lots of notes.
11. Use an electronic organizer.
12. Establish a routine.
13. Ask questions again and again until you understand.
14. Study with a partner.
15. Take all the time you can for a test.
16. Ask professors to give a test study guide.
17. Get a head start on your reading.
18. Do more than is required.
19. Give yourself rewards.
20. Start research papers early.

"CLAYBORN! THIS IS INDEED A SURPRISE!"

Reprinted by permission: Frank Cotham

21. Take hard classes in the summer.
22. Parent yourself.
23. Be accountable for yourself.
24. Trick your mind into thinking you like something even if you don't.
25. Go to summer school.
26. Read all your assignments.
27. Fight the odds.

28. Burn an assignment into your brain. Live it, breathe it, think it; let it become a part of you.
29. Divide large projects into small steps.
30. Read information on university bulletin boards.
31. Spend lots of time studying. It works!
32. Study smart.
33. Be patient. It all works out.
34. Relax.
35. Make lots of friends.
36. Develop a good attitude.
37. Be pleasant and polite.
38. Work hard. College can sneak up on you!
39. Get work experience.
40. Take aptitude and interest tests.
41. Do internships.
42. Be confident.
43. Be sure your professors know you by name.
44. Be realistic.
45. Balance work with recreation and pleasure.
46. Approach each semester as a fresh beginning.
47. Travel and get a global perspective.
48. Attend all classes.
49. Demonstrate a sense of confidence.
50. Avoid complaining.
51. Resist the easy way out.
52. Keep things in proper perspective.
53. Learn from everyone.
54. Use the resources of the university.
55. Read the university newspaper.
56. Recognize your limitations.
57. Learn how the system works.
58. Understand that the university is not against you.
59. Try and fail but never fail to try.
60. Be resourceful.
61. Explore all the avenues that are available.
62. Expand your horizons.
63. Get good grades.

64. Pretend the professor is going to give you a daily quiz.
65. Remember that learning is a process. Enjoy the journey.
66. Face your anxieties.
67. Avoid procrastination.
68. Know your learning styles.
69. See it! Say it! Do it!
70. Use multisensory learning strategies.
71. Use the library.
72. Resolve past hurts. They interfere with learning.
73. Find a listening friend.
74. Do your best; always give more than the rest.
75. Study even if you don't have specific homework.
76. Being too social can be the death of good grades.
77. Remember you're attending college to get an education.
78. Choose extracurricular activities that will enhance your career.
79. Learn how to use technology.
80. Survive your freshman year.
81. Practice making up examinations.
82. Make up essay questions. Write the answers.
83. Take tests backwards.
84. Find a way that works for you and stick to it.
85. Get to know your professors.
86. Sit where the professor will see you.
87. Study to remember.
88. Overlearn.
89. Learn from those who do well.
90. Emulate good role models.
91. Attend university events and seminars.
92. Study just before sleeping.
93. Get to know other students in your classes.
94. Study as if you are the professor who will be giving the lecture.
95. Pray for wisdom.
96. Keep track of your grades. Be in charge of your achievements.
97. Demonstrate good listening skills.

"With all due respect for circumstance, I'd like to launch directly into extended pomp."

98. Show appreciation.

99. Perform community service.

100. Recognize the extraordinary nature of the college experience. Never again will you be in a little society as unique in composition and purpose. College is a microcosm of life. It is an opportunity to build a foundation for living that will stand the test of time.

Graduation!

Congratulations! You Have Met All the Requirements for Graduation!

1. Fill out application to graduate!
2. Pick up cap and gown!
3. Shout hallelujah!
4. Tell everyone you know!
5. Send invitations!
6. Thank your professors!
7. Get a job!
8. Pay back loans!
9. Clean your room!
10. Be proud! You did it!

References

Aaron, P.G., and Catherine Baker. (1991). *Reading disabilities in college and high school: Diagnosis and management.* Parkton: York Press.

Armstrong, William H., and M. Willard Lampe II. (1983). *Study tips.* Woodbury: Barron's Educational Series, Inc.

Annis, Linda Ferrill. (1983). *Study techniques.* Dubuque: Wm. C. Brown Company.

Beaumont, J. Graham. (1989). *Brain power.* New York: Harper and Row.

Begley, Sharon. Memory. *Newsweek.* (September, 1986): pp. 48–54.

Bliss, Edwin. (1976). *Getting things done.* New York: Bantam Books.

Brinckerhoff, Loring C., Stan F. Shaw, and Joan M. McGuire. (1993). *Promoting postsecondary education for students with learning disabilities.* Austin: PRO-ED, Inc.

Brown, James I. (1980). *Programmed vocabulary: The CPD approach.* Englewood Cliffs: Prentice-Hall.

Carlson, Neil R. (1993). *Psychology: The science of behavior.* (4th ed.) Boston: Allyn and Bacon, Inc.

Carnegie, Dale. (1936). *How to win friends and influence people.* New York: Simon and Schuster.

Cherry, Clare, Douglas Godwin, and Jesse Staples. (1989). *Is the left brain always right?* Belmont: Fearon Teacher Aids.

Central Michigan University. (1993). *1993–94 Bulletin.* Vol. 99, No. 3, Mt. Pleasant, MI.

Craik, F., and M. Watkins. (1973). The Role of Rehearsal in Short-Term Memory. *Journal of Verbal Learning and Verbal Behavior.* 12: 599–607.

Culp, Stephanie. (1986). *How to get organized when you don't have the time.* Cincinnati: Writer's Digest Books.

Devine, Thomas G. (1987). *Teaching study skills: A guide for teachers.* Newton: Allyn and Bacon, Inc.

Dunn, Rita, and Kenneth Dunn. (1993). *Teaching students to read through their individual learning style.* Boston: Allyn and Bacon.

Ehrlich, Ida. (1986). *Instant vocabulary.* New York: Pocket Books.

Ellis, David B. (1991). *Becoming a master student,* 6th ed. Rapid City: College Survival, Inc.

Flippo, Rona F., and David C. Caverly, eds. (1991). *Teaching reading and study strategies at the college level.* Newark: International Reading Assoc.

Hamachek, Alice L. (1989). Study Strategies for the Secondary Student: Enhancing Memory. *Michigan Reading Journal.* 22: 22–26. Grand Rapids: Michigan Reading Assoc.

Hamachek, Alice L. (1990). *Interactive reading-teaching model, secondary reading: A new direction for the future.* Grand Rapids: Michigan Reading Assoc.

Hamachek, Alice L., and Frank A. Stancato. (1990). The Interactive Nature and Reciprocal Effects of Cognitive and Affective Learning. *Education.* 3(1): 77–81. Appleton: Peterson Press.

Healy, Jane M. (1990). *Endangered minds.* NY: Simon and Schuster.

Irwin, Judith W., and Isabel Baker. (1989). *Promoting active reading comprehension strategies.* Boston: Allyn and Bacon.

Johnson, Dale D., and P. David Pearson. (1984). *Teaching reading vocabulary,* 2nd ed. New York: Holt, Rinehart and Winston.

Kesselman-Turkel, and Franklynn Peterson. (1981). *Test-taking strategies.* Chicago: Contemporary Books, Inc.

Kirk, Samuel A., and James C. Chalfant. (1984). *Academic and developmental learning disabilities.* Columbus: Love Publishing.

Landy, Frank J. (1984). *Psychology: The science of people.* Englewood Cliffs: Prentice-Hall, Inc.

Lengefeld, Uelaine. (1987). *Study skills strategies.* Los Altos: Crisp Publications.

Levine, Melvin D. (1987). *Developmental variation and learning disorders.* Cambridge: Educators Publishing Service, Inc.

Lorayne, Harry, and Jerry Lucas. (1974). *The memory book.* New York: Ballantine Books.

Michaels, Craig A. et al. (1988). *From high school to college: Keys to success for students with learning disabilities.* Alberston: Human Resources Center.

Miller, George. (1956). The Magical Number Seven: Plus or Minus Two. *Psychological Review.* 63: 81–97.

Minninger, Joan. (1984). *Total recall.* Emmanus: Rodale Press.

Olney, Claude W., J.D. (1988). *Where there's a will there's a way.* Paoli: American Educational Publishers.

Ornstein, Robert, and Richard F. Thompson. (1984). *The amazing brain.* Boston: Houghton Mifflin Co.

Restak, Richard. (1984). *The brain.* New York: Bantam Books.

Robinson, F. (1941). *Effective study.* New York: Harper and Row.

Rose, Colin. (1985). *Accelerated learning.* London: Topaz Publishing Ltd.

Russell, Peter. (1979). *The brain book.* New York: Penguin Books.

Scheiber, Barbara, and Jeanne Talpers. (1987). *Unlocking potential.* Bethesda: Adler and Adler, Publishers, Inc.

Seligman, Martin. (1990). *Learned optimism.* New York: Pocket Books.

Sedita, Joan. (1989). *Landmark study skills guide.* Prides Crossing: Landmark Foundation.

Seleebey, William M. (1981). *Study skills for success.* National Publishers of the Black Hills, Inc.

Seward, S. S., Jr. (1910). *Notetaking.* Boston: Allyn and Bacon.

Shepherd, James F. (1987). *College vocabulary skills.* Boston: Houghton Mifflin Company.

Shepherd, James F. (1981). *RSVP The Houghton Mifflin reading, studying & vocabulary program.* Boston: Houghton Mifflin Company.

Tulving, E. (1962). The Effect of Alphabetical Subjective Organization of Memorizing Unrelated Words. *Canadian Journal of Psychology.* 16: 185–191.

Vail, Priscilla L. (1987). *Smart kids with school problems.* New York: E.P.Dutton.

Wonder, Jacquelyn, and Priscilla Donovan. (1984). *Whole-brain thinking.* New York: William Morrow and Co.

Zechmeister, Eugene B., and Stanley E. Nyberg. (1982). *Human memory: An introduction to research and theory.* Monterey: Brooks/Cole Publishing Company.

Index